As the Sand Shifts

*Reevaluating the U.S. Strategy
in the Middle East*

Riad Aisami, PhD

ISBN: 978-1-969880-69-8

Dedication

To Leyla, Lamees, and Lena.

Contents

Table of Figures

About the Author and the Book

Dr. Riad Aisami is a distinguished scholar and Professor Emeritus. He has made notable contributions to the field of U.S.-Middle East relations through his research and published works. Drawing on his strategic analysis and firsthand experience, this book examines U.S. policy in the Middle East and the forces that have shaped it.

Integrating insights from a decade-spanning collection of articles and strategic analyses, Dr. Aisami challenges readers to reconsider long-held assumptions and calls for a new U.S. role in the Middle East that moves beyond militarized strategies of the Cold War toward a more constructive and forward-looking engagement.

While this book is not explicitly crafted as academic work, it is, however, designed to function as a resource for fostering discussions among college and university students. It aims to serve as a tool for stimulating critical thinking and providing accessible insights for students engaging in conversations on crucial geopolitical topics. More importantly, by offering perspectives on significant issues, the book aspires to significantly contribute to the intellectual development of students, encouraging thoughtful dialogue and analysis within the academic setting.

Preface

Over the past seven years, I have published two pivotal Arabic books that delve into the intricate relationship between the United States and the Middle East. The first, "Obama Departs and Leaves the Middle East in Flames," was a timely warning published on January 1, 2017, three weeks before President Obama's exit from the White House. Its follow-up, "The United States and the Evolving Events in the Middle East: The Geostrategic Global Revelry and the New World Order," released in mid-2022, expands on these urgent themes, highlighting an ever-evolving crisis. My latest work, "As the Sand Shifts," offers a thorough and updated lens on the last Arabic edition of my previous book. It meticulously investigates America's involvement in the Middle East since World War II, dissecting five pressing issues: the Arab-Israeli conflict, Iran's nuclear ambitions and regional assertiveness, the rising Russian challenge, the competitive dynamics with China, and the devastating conflict in Syria. Through the lens of strategic planning, I confront four essential questions: Where are we now? How did we reach this crossroads? Where are we heading? Most crucially, how do we forge a better future? This intent is not just an academic exercise; it is a call to action. Instead of merely recounting history, I draw on insights from the social sciences—geography, history, economics, and political theory—to illuminate future pathways and prescribe actionable strategies tailored to today's challenges.

This book has undergone rigorous peer review by esteemed experts in political science, affirming its depth and factual reliability. The Middle East is not merely a region—it is the world's foremost geostrategic battleground, shaped by global powers and laden with both profound potential and dire conflict. For more than three decades, the United States has wielded dominant influence in this region. Yet, as challenges from Russia and China intensify, we must abandon outdated Cold War strategies that no longer serve us. It is time for a bold, transformative approach to reclaim our place as a global leader. As an American citizen with deep roots in the Middle East, I am not just a spectator; I am invested in the future I envision for both the United States and the wider world. Our collective survival depends on engaging with these pressing issues now more than ever. I fervently hope this book reaches a vast audience—this will be my true measure of success. After all, as the Chinese proverb wisely warns, "A closed book is nothing but a pile of paper."

Riad S. Aisami

Augusta, Georgia, November 2023

Introduction

History Does Not Make Events; Events Make History

History goes through stages. Each stage begins and ends with critical events. The stage ends when the occurring events are too big to fit within its dynamic structure. The most recent historical era began with the global upheaval of World War II (1939-1945), during which the U.S. played a pivotal role, despite its late entry. Following the war, a prolonged period of geopolitical tension, known as the Cold War (1947-1991), unfolded between the United States and the Soviet Union, resulting in U.S. victory.

Transitioning into the late 20th century, the U.S. got involved in a significant conflict in the Middle East. The Gulf War (1990-1991) was triggered by Iraq's invasion of Kuwait, leading to U.S. and Allied intervention. In the early 2000s, the landscape shifted again with the onset of the War on Terror. Prompted by the 9/11 attacks in 2001, the U.S. engaged in military operations in Afghanistan and Iraq, marking a significant chapter in global geopolitics. These events, spanning from World War II to the War on Terror, have shaped the trajectory of international relations, underscoring the U.S.'s role in pivotal historical moments.

However, the election of Barack Obama in 2008 marked a significant historical moment, symbolizing a shift since the end of the Cold War. During his presidency, global events unfolded, including the Arab Spring uprising in the Middle East and North

Africa (MENA) that began in late 2010 in Tunisia and spread to Egypt, Libya, Syria, and Yemen. Undoubtedly, the Arab Spring marked a turning point, signaling the first stage of failure of the previous historical phase in the Middle East and having an impact worldwide. Despite President Obama's call for a change in the Middle East and North Africa with political reforms and democratic transformation, his efforts encountered strong resistance. Authoritarian regimes in the Middle East, such as in Syria and Iran, and Monarchies in the region, including Saudi Arabia and Jordan, opposed Obama's proposed changes, as did global totalitarian regimes like China, Russia, and North Korea. Even Israel, the region's only democracy, resisted it, fearing potential impacts on its unique status. This collective resistance led to regional and global conflict, and the intended democratic changes in the Middle East failed. Such a resistance bolstered authoritarian regimes and paved the way for the emergence of more dangerous organizations, such as the Islamic State in Iraq and Syria (ISIS), in 2014. Consequently, the United States shifted its Middle East objective from promoting democracy to combating ISIS in a global war in Syria and Iraq.

In my book "Obama Departs and Leaves the Middle East in Flames," I characterized the fight against ISIS and the international and regional conflict in and on Syria as a potential spark for a Third World War. I also emphasized that this conflict would differ significantly from the two preceding world wars, citing distinctions like the nature of this conflict, the key players involved, the battlegrounds, and the types of weaponry to be deployed[1]. In a letter to President Harry S. Truman, Albert Einstein warned: "I know not with what weapons World War III will be fought, but World War IV will be fought with sticks and stones"[2].

The Middle East has been a sought-after region throughout history due to its strategic location, vital waterways, and abundant natural resources, particularly oil. After World War I, Great Britain and France secured their interests in the Middle East through the Sykes-Picot Agreement, which led to the colonization of the region for over three decades. Post-World War II, the United States consolidated its influence in the Middle East by establishing the State of Israel in Palestine. Like Great Britain used the Balfour Declaration to advance its colonial agenda in the Middle East, the U.S. leveraged Israel to bolster its global superpower status in the Middle East. The American perceived objectives for creating Israel included, but were not limited to:

- Preventing the Arab World from being united.

- Asserting dominance in Middle Eastern politics.

- Securing the flow of the Gulf oil.

---

[1] Aisami, R. (January 01, 2017). "Obama is Departing, and the Middle East is in Flames," Arabic Scientific Publishers, Inc., Beirut, Lebanon, 2017.

[2] Johnson, A. (April 15, 2005). "The Culture of Einstein" Time Magazine. https://www.nbcnews.com/id/wbna7406337.

- Gaining leverage in the conflict with the Soviet Union.

Given the evolving global geopolitical landscape and the rise of new competitors, such as Russia and China, the U.S. needs to reassess its Middle East strategy and recalibrate its policies. While U.S. policies in the Middle East have evolved since World War II, the strategic approach has remained unchanged. It remains the same as if the Soviet Union still existed and the Cold War was still lingering. Thus, the United States must redirect its approach to the Middle East by maintaining a significant presence in West Asia (the Middle East) and reevaluate its strategy to adapt to the novel changes and succeed in the current international competition, especially against rivals like Russia and China. Additionally, it should assume a new role in fostering unity and cooperation in the region to counter the potential threat of China's emerging dominance. This approach should parallel the post-World War II strategy in Western Europe, where the United States played a pivotal role in unifying the region against the Soviet Union's influence over Eastern Europe. This approach has become essential for navigating the emerging "Third World War" and effectively competing with China, which has been identified as the primary adversary in contemporary geopolitics.

After World War II, the United States supported Israel as a critical ally in the Middle East to advance its dominance and counter the Soviet Union. When the Soviets invaded Afghanistan in 1979, the U.S. used the new Islamic regime in Iran as a buffer against the Soviet influence in the region. However, the geopolitical landscape has undergone significant changes since then. The Soviet Union collapsed due to its involvement in Afghanistan, and the eight-year Iran-Iraq War in the '80s drained both countries. In the '90s, after the Gulf War, the U.S. pursued a dual containment policy against Iraq and Iran. However, at the beginning of the 21st century, U.S. presidents implemented varying foreign policy approaches toward the two countries. President George W. Bush pursued a preemptive strike policy, leading to the U.S. occupation of Afghanistan and Iraq[3]. President Obama adopted a no-war approach and called for withdrawal from both countries. However, he ordered the assassination of Osama Bin Laden, the Al-Qaeda leader[4].

President Trump introduced the "Make America Great Again" (MAGA) slogan and diverged from President Obama's peaceful stance and President Bush's preemptive war doctrine. However, his administration unilaterally withdrew from the Iran Nuclear Agreement, which was signed by President Obama's administration in 2015. He also ordered the killing of Qassim Soleimani, the Commander of Al-Quds Brigade of the Iranian Revolutionary Guard (IRG), and Abu Baker al-Baghdadi, the first caliph of the Islamic State in Iraq and Syria (ISIS). Also, his administration negotiated the withdrawal of U.S. troops from

---

[3] National Security Strategy, October 2022. Retrieved 8-November-Combined-PDF-for-Upload.pdf (whitehouse.gov).

[4] Barack Obama Foreign Affairs. Iraq and Afghanistan. Michael Nelson, Professor of Political Science at Rhodes College, UVA, Miller Center, 2023. Retrieved from: Barack Obama: Foreign Affairs | Miller Center.

Afghanistan with the Taliban[5]. President Biden reversed many of President Trump's foreign policies but did not fully embrace President Obama's no-war approach. His administration retained critical aspects of Obama's policies, such as supporting the two-state solution for the Israeli-Palestinian conflict and not opposing President Trump's Abraham Accords to normalize relations between Israel and key Arab states. Notably, President Biden's administration swiftly withdrew U.S. troops from Afghanistan, leaving room for the Taliban's return to power. Additionally, his administration expanded the American presence in Iraq, diverging from Obama's approach, despite Biden's earlier association with that administration[6].

Despite these changes in the United States administrations, the U.S. has not been able to establish a coherent and effective foreign policy in the Middle East since the end of the Cold War that maintains its national security interests. In a strategic research study conducted by the RAND Center for Middle East Public Policy in 2021, the researchers concluded that "U.S. policy in the Middle

---

[5] Afghan Conflict: Trump hails deal with Taliban to end 18-year war. ABC, February 29, 2020, 04:12 pm ET. Retrieved from: Afghan conflict: Trump hails deal with Taliban to end 18-year war (bbc.com).

[6] Biden Defends Decision to Pull Troops from Afghanistan Despite Resurgent Taliban. NPR, July 8, 2021, 3:18 pm ET. Retrieved from: Biden Defends Decision to Pull U.S. Troops from Afghanistan: NPR.

East across successive administrations, on balance, failed to produce positive results for American interests or the region"[7].

The Middle East is the most significant geostrategic region in the world, historically shaped by global powers. The United States has been the sole dominant power in the Middle East for over three decades since the end of the Cold War. Today, challenges from Russia and China necessitate a fresh perspective that transcends the outdated strategies of the Cold War. By understanding past mistakes and adopting a forward-thinking approach, the United States can successfully navigate the Middle East's complexities and safeguard America's position on the world stage.

This book provides a comprehensive overview of American Middle East policies, drawing on the author's firsthand experiences in the Middle East and the United States. It synthesizes various sources, incorporating prior publications and a decade-spanning collection of articles and strategic analyses. It focuses on five critical issues confronting the United States in the Middle East, which are significant in shaping the new world order, including the Arab-Israeli Conflict, Iran's nuclear program and regional influence, the Russian challenge, competition with China, and the proxy war in Syria. These five issues are presented in chapters three to seven, respectively. Chapter eight includes a recap summary,

---

[7] RAND 2021Study Report. Dalia Dasa Kaye, Linda Robinson, Jeffrey Martini, Nathan Vest, and Ashley L. Rhoads. "Reimagining U.S. Strategy in the Middle East: Sustainable Partnerships, Strategic Investments." RAND Corporation, Santa Monica, Calif, 2021, Introduction, Page 1 .

conclusions, and offers recommendations for rethinking a U.S. Strategy in the Middle East during the pressing war in Gaza and beyond. It advocates for an innovative approach that departs from the Cold War-era militarized Grand Strategy to a Soft Power Strategy (Smart Diplomacy): A selective, creative, and sensitive strategy (SCSS). This alternative strategy is primarily inspired by President Obama's Middle East and North Africa Approach, as summarized in Chapter Two, following a historical background of the region's importance and the conflicts over it presented in Chapter One.

Chapter 1: The U.S. and the Middle East

Historical Background

Geography Makes History, and Economy Directs Politics.

The Middle East is often regarded as the heart of the world, and whoever controls the heart maintains the body. Therefore, the pursuit of control over the Middle East by powerful states, dating back to the dawn of history, predates the United States' victory in World War II. Such a situation existed before the United States' founding and even before the continent's discovery. The struggle for Middle East dominance involved Europe, primarily Great Britain and France, against the Ottoman Empire. This conflict, in turn, prompted exploration and led to the discovery of the South and North American continents. In 1492, Christopher Columbus proposed an exploratory cruise to European kings, mainly King Ferdinand II and Queen Isabella II, the Catholic Monarchs of Spain, to find an alternative route to East Asia to bypass Muslim territories[8]. The reason for this voyage lies in the Ottoman Empire's

---

[8] History Resources. Columbus Reports on His First Voyage, 1493. A Spotlight on a Primary Source by Christopher Columbus. The Gilder Lehrman Institute of American History.

https://www.gilderlehrman.org/history-resources/spotlight-primary-source/columbus-reports-his-first-voyage-1493.

control over the region, which extended from the Caucasus in the East to the Balkans in the West. The Ottoman Empire, ruling in the name of the Islamic Caliphate for more than six centuries (1299-1923), held sway over this extensive territory[9], as shown in Fig. 1 below.

Fig 1 for the Ottoman Empire Map

Figure 1 Ottoman Empire Map

The Middle East, situated in a strategically important geographic location and traversed by vital waterways, has historically drawn states and empires seeking power through geostrategic expansion. Key water passages include the Suez Canal

---

[9] Ottoman Empire Decline and Definitions. By History.com Editors. Published on: Ottoman Empire - WWI, Decline & Definition | HISTORY.

(connecting the Mediterranean and Red Seas), the Bab al-Mandab Strait (linking the Red Sea to the Arabian Sea, facilitating access to the Indian and Atlantic Oceans), and the Strait of Hormuz (separating the Arabian Peninsula from Iran, connecting the Arabian Sea to the Gulf of Oman). The Suez Canal, a notably crucial endeavor, was Egypt's pioneering effort to establish a vital East-West water route, connecting the Mediterranean Sea in Port Said to the Red Sea in Suez City[10], as shown in Fig. below.

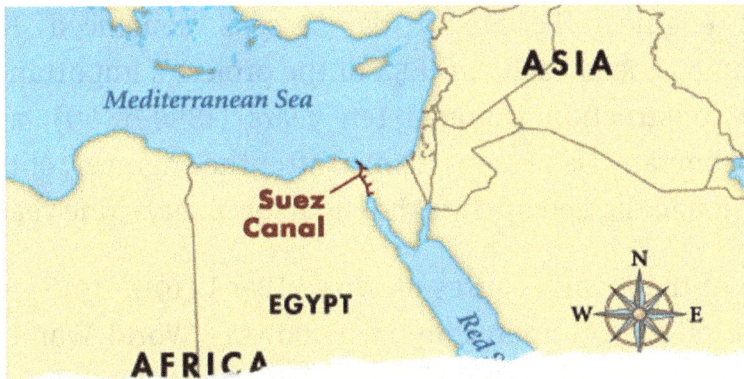

Fig. 2 for the Suez Canal Map

Figure 2 Suez Canal Map

The idea of linking the Mediterranean and Red Seas goes back over four thousand years, originating in the era of the Pharaohs. The notion of digging the Suez Canal for logistical purposes has ancient roots. Throughout history, the canal has been opened and

---

[10] Strategic Geography of the Middle East. Hoover Institute. Published on: Strategic Geography of The Middle East | Hoover Institution Strategic Geography of The Middle East.

closed for assorted reasons, including natural factors like siltation, and for military, political, and economic considerations. A significant closure occurred in 760 AD when Abbasid Caliph Abu Jaffar al-Mansur ordered it to disrupt supplies to rebels[11].

Napoleon attempted to reopen the canal during the French campaign against Egypt in 1798-1801, but technical issues and the failure of his campaign halted the effort. Despite Napoleon's death in 1821, the French continued their pursuit to reopen the canal. French engineer Ferdinand de Lesseps convinced Khedive Muhammad Saeed Pasha in 1854 of the project's importance. The canal's construction spanned ten years (1859-1869), and the French company De Lesseps, named after the engineer, obtained a concession to dig and operate the canal for ninety-nine years[12].

One of the pivotal causes of World War I (1914-1918) was the collapse of the Ottoman Empire. Following World War I, Great Britain and France assumed control of the Ottoman Empire's legacy in the region. The French company De Lesseps continued to manage the Suez Canal in collaboration with Great Britain, which exerted influence over Egypt, Palestine, and Jordan. However, this

---

[11] For 152 years, eight previous closures of the Suez Canal. Retrieved from: www.skynewsarbia.com.

[12] Suez Canal Overview. Published on: SCA - SCA Overview (suezcanal.gov.eg).

arrangement persisted until President Gamal Abdel Nasser of Egypt nationalized the canal in 1956 [13].

Following World War II, the United States forcefully entered the Middle East, leading to the gradual decline and ultimate loss of influence by Great Britain and France in the region. This situation notably culminated in the Suez War of 1956, which led to the British and French withdrawal from Egypt and the Middle East, marking the end of the old colonial system.

Unlike England and France after World War I, the United States did not directly occupy the Middle East after World War II. Instead, President Harry Truman's Administration pursued a strategy of supporting military and authoritarian regimes in the region that were friendly to the U.S. to safeguard Israel's security and advance its interests in the area. Hence, in 1949, upon its establishment, the CIA backed a military coup in Syria led by Chief Military Leader Hosny Al-Zaim, effectively ousting the elected president, Shukri al-Quwatli, and ending the first parliamentary system in the region[14]. Also, the United States did not oppose the 1952 coup in Egypt, which the Egyptian Free Officers performed. Egypt was the most important country in the Middle East over which the United States needed to exert influence to advance its new Middle East

---

[13] . Suez Canal by History.com Editors. Published on: Suez Canal - Crisis, Location & Egypt | HISTORY.

[14] Based on Miles Copeland's Book "The Game of Nation: The Amorality of Power Politics." Simon and Schuster, 1969, p. 73).

strategy. "The Free Officers coup of 1952 gave the Americans an incentive toward realizing their objective in the region"[15]. However, the United States had a rocky start with Gamal Abdel Nasser, the new Egyptian leader who became a national symbol in the Arab World and called for the Non-Aligned Movement, which in general favored the Soviet Union over the United States.

Iran was also a critical country in the Middle East. The United States could not afford to lose its support in the oil market and its struggle with the Soviet Union. Therefore, "in 1953, President Eisenhower ordered the CIA to depose Mohammed Mossadegh, the popular, elected leader of the Iranian parliament and an ardent nationalist who opposed British and American influence in Iran. The coup severely tarnished America's reputation among Iranians, who lost trust in American claims of protecting democracy"[16].

The American involvement in the Middle East primarily centered on two key issues: Oil and Israel. This theme persisted from President Harry S. Truman to George W. Bush, reflecting a

_____

[15] American Support for the 1952 Egyptian Coup: Why? Laila Amin Morsy. Middle Eastern Studies. Vol. 31, No. 2 (Apr. 1995), pp. 307-316. Published By: Taylor & Francis, Ltd.

[16] U.S. Policy in the Middle East: 1949-2008. By Pierre Tristam. Updated on July 30, 2019. Retrieved from U.S. Policy in the Middle East: A Brief History (thoughtco.com).

consistent focus on these strategic priorities."[17] However, with President Obama's election in 2008, the significance of oil began to diminish compared to previous administrations. During Obama's tenure, his administration experienced a shift in the U.S. oil strategy. The country was then prepared to release its oil reserves, reaching the highest levels in 2012 with a recorded increase of 4.5 billion barrels to 33.4 billion, the highest since 1976[18]. The rate of growth peaked in early 2016 with the approval of shale oil extraction, known as fracking[19]. Additionally, the Obama administration initiated a gradual transition towards alternative energy, aiming to peak by 2030. However, oil fracking was controversial among Americans and across the political spectrum in Washington[20], and the Republicans contested President Obama's energy policy[21].

---

[17] Toby Craig Jones. America, Oil, and War in the Middle East. The Journal of American History, Volume 99, Issue 1, June 12, 2012, Pages 208-218. https://doi.org/10.1093/jahist/jas045

[18] U.S. Energy Information Administration. Annual Report, September 2012.

[19] Mark Lasky. The Outlook of U.S. Production of Shell Oil. Congressional Budget Office. Working Paper. May 2016. Retrieved from: The Outlook for U.S. Production of Shale Oil (cbo.gov).

[20] America Split on Support for Fracking in Oil, Natural Gas. By Art Swift. GALLUP, March 23, 2015. Retrieved from: Americans Split on Support for Fracking in Oil, Natural Gas (gallup.com/

[21] Romney vs. Obama and U.S. Energy Policy. By Rawi Abdelal and Kaitlyn Tuthill, Faculty and Research. Harvard Business School, October 2012.

Despite the U.S. growing energy independence President Obama conceived in his second term, the Middle East remained a primary source of global oil (more than half of global proved reserves and 35.5% of global production in 2019), and 13% of world trade passed through the Suez Canal[22]. A Statistical Review of World Energy-2021 reveals that the Middle East accounts for 31% of global oil production, 18% of gas, 48% of proved oil reserves, and 40% of gas proved reserves[23].

President Obama fulfilled his campaign promise to withdraw American troops from Iraq, a decision criticized by Republicans, who deemed it premature to relinquish energy interests in the Middle East. While the protection of Israel has been an ongoing and intricate issue since its inception in 1948, it remains unresolved. Over the past seventy-five years, the United States has struggled to find a lasting solution to this conflict. The current turmoil, wars, and divisions in the Middle East reflect the unresolved nature of this conflict. Unfortunately, the area's geostrategic location, which features vital waterways that connect the East and West and serve as a land bridge linking Asia and Africa, makes a peaceful resolution unlikely without a change in the U.S. policy toward Israel and the

---

Retrieved from: Romney vs. Obama and U.S. Energy Policy - Case - Faculty & Research - Harvard Business School (hbs.eu/)

[22] Oil prices remain volatile aimed uncertainty arising from geopolitical conflict Paolo Agnolucci and Kaltrina Tema. World Bang Blogs, January 4, 2024. Retrieved from: Oil prices remain volatile amid uncertainty arising from geopolitical conflict (worldbank.org).

[23] Retrieved on January 12, 2024, from Statistical Review of World Energy 2021 – Middle East (bp.com)

entire Middle East. In the mid-fifties of the last century, Egyptian President Gamal Abdel Nasser offered reconciliation in response to U.S. President Dwight Eisenhower's project. Nasser proposed border amendments, seeking a land connection between Egypt and Jordan through the Negev Desert. This was rejected by Israeli Prime Minister David Ben-Gurion, who opposed conceding land for peace, stating it was akin to suicide[24].

In the aftermath of the 1967 war, Israel gained control of all Palestinian territories, including Gaza, the West Bank, and East Jerusalem. Also, it expanded into neighboring Arab lands, occupying the Sinai Peninsula from Egypt and the Golan Heights from Syria. Following these events, Resolution No. 242 was passed by the United Nations, urging Israel to relinquish the occupied territories in exchange for peace. However, this resolution did not yield the desired results. Following the 1973 War, the United Nations passed Resolution No. 338, urging an immediate ceasefire. Despite this UN resolution, hostilities persisted. In response, two subsequent resolutions, 339 and 340, were enacted with the assistance of the Soviet Union. The escalating international pressure eventually led to a cessation of hostilities, prompting Israel to enter into a formal ceasefire agreement with both Egypt and Syria[25].

---

[24] How Egypt's Gamal Abdel Nasser Changed World Politics. By Joel Beinin. Published on 11/02/202. Retrieved from: How Egypt's Gamal Abdel Nasser Changed World Politics (jacobin.com)

[25] ADL. Backgrounder. United Nations Security Resolutions 2423/338. Retrieved from: https://www.adl.org/resources/backgrounder/united-

While this development did not immediately alter the broader dynamics of the Arab-Israeli conflict, it played a pivotal role in shaping the trajectory of a future peace process. Notably, the groundwork laid by these events became instrumental in the eventual peace negotiations between Egypt and Israel. These negotiations culminated in a significant agreement in 1979, where Israel agreed to return the entire Sinai Peninsula to Egypt in exchange for lasting peace. This agreement marked a crucial turning point in the region, demonstrating the potential for diplomatic solutions to long-standing conflicts in the Middle East.

In 1993, the Oslo Accords were introduced, presenting a framework for a two-state solution[26]. Nevertheless, a significant geographic challenge emerged, with Gaza separated from the West Bank by Israeli territory. **Yitzhak Rabin,** who was Israel's prime minister in the early 1990s, once infamously said: "I wish I could wake up one day and find that Gaza has sunk into the sea"[27]. Therefore, the Israeli government remains elusive on what to do with Gaza since withdrawing from it in 2005, and the ongoing war illustrates this fact. Gaza is a geographical obstacle that makes the

---

nations-security-council-resolution-242338#:~:text=Resolution%20242%20(reaffirmed%20in%20338,peace%20treaties%20in%20the%20region.

[26] Office of the Historian. The Oslo Accords and the Arab Israeli Process. Retrieved from: https://history.state.gov/milestones/1993-2000/oslo.

[27] Laying Siege to Gaza is No Solution. By Yousef Muneer. Foreign Policy, October 9, 2023. Retrieved from: Israel's Invasion of Gaza Could Yield Mass Atrocities, Genocide Against Palestinians (foreignpolicy.com).

success of the two-state solution contingent upon considerations such as land exchange or redrawing the map. Fig. 3 below illustrates this situation on the map.

Figure No. 3

Figure 3 The Gaza Strip Location on the Map

In summary, the Middle East has experienced significant shifts in its geopolitical landscape since World War I. These changes began with the Balfour Declaration and direct British involvement in the region post-World War I in 1919. Following World War II, the United States assumed a prominent role in 19949, particularly with the establishment of Israel in 1948.

The region saw further upheaval with the Iranian Islamic Revolution in 1979 and the Iraq-Iran War (1980-1988). The fall of the Berlin Wall and the collapse of the Soviet Union marked a significant global shift, which also impacted the Middle East. The Gulf War in 1991, triggered by Iraq's invasion of Kuwait, and the subsequent War on Terrorism following the events of September 11, 2001, led to the occupation of Afghanistan and Iraq. However, the election of President Barack Obama in 2008 and his 2009 Middle East Initiative signaled a new chapter in the Middle East. In his book Shifting Sands: The United States in the Middle East, Joel S. Migdal refers to these transformative events from 1919 to 2009 as "every thirty-year geopolitical landscape change[28].

In 2009, President Obama launched his ambitious and comprehensive Middle East and North Africa (MENA) Initiative. This comprehensive approach was designed to address the long-standing Palestinian-Israeli conflict and broader issues within the Middle East. The initiative's scope extended beyond territorial disputes, focusing on fostering solutions to regional challenges, including promoting democracy and political reforms. This book focuses on the first attempt at a shift in U.S. Strategy in the Middle East, initiated by President Barack Obama, which distinguished it from all attempts by his predecessors, the American Presidents from President Truman to President George W. Bush. Therefore, the next chapter, Chapter Two, presents an exclusive summary of President Obama's Middle East Initiative and investigates the reasons behind its ultimate failure. Chapter Three provides an

---

[28] Migdal, J. S. (2014). Shifting Sands: The United States in the Middle East. Columbia University Press, 2014.

overview of all other initiatives and peace processes and explicitly addresses the Palestinian-Israeli dispute as an integral part of the broader Arab-Israeli conflict. By situating this issue within the larger regional context, the author aims to provide a nuanced understanding of the complexities that contributed to President Obama's challenges in implementing his Middle East initiative.

Chapter 2: Obama and the New Middle East Approach

History does not Make Great People, But Great People Make History.

The Arab Spring uprisings, which began in late 2010, had significant implications for Barack Obama during his first six years as the forty-fourth president (2009-2015). During this period, it offered a pivotal opportunity for Obama to influence not only the Arab world and the Middle East but also the global landscape. Successfully navigating this situation could have solidified his legacy as a transformative leader, particularly given his historic 2008 election as the first African American president.

Barack Obama's appeal, rooted in his African heritage and upbringing in the world's largest Muslim country, Indonesia, resonated globally. His campaign slogan, "Yes, We Can," inspired unprecedented engagement from American youth in the political process. Additionally, Obama's charisma and determination were evident in his famous phrase, contributing to his successful bid for the presidency. The Arab Spring presented a fertile ground for President Obama to extend the seeds of change he had sown in the United States. His pivotal speech, "A New Beginning," delivered at Cairo University in 2009, had a profound impact on Arab youth. Over the following two years, this influence manifested as countless young Arabs took to the streets, demanding freedom, and change from long-standing dictatorial regimes. The potential of the Arab Spring to transform the region and the impact on Obama's presidency were significant. Had it achieved its intended transformation, Obama could have emerged as a global champion of change and freedom, solidifying his position as the leader of the free world. This missed opportunity remains significant in assessing Obama's presidency in the broader context of global events during his 8-year tenure.

In his book "The World as It Is," Ben Rhodes, President Obama's Deputy National Security Advisor and Confidant, highlighted that "Obama brought a distinct worldview to the presidency. This worldview differed from that of his predecessors and the White male individuals who typically held elevated national security positions. Obama's perspective aimed to address the intricate nuances of U.S. foreign policy"[29].

Early in his political life, Barack Obama shared the views of other intellectual elites in the United States, advocating for new policies and strategies in the post-Cold War era following the events of 1989, the fall of the Berlin Wall, and 1991, the collapse of the Soviet Union[1]. He recognized, however, that addressing the remnants of the Cold War required tackling terrorism, particularly in the aftermath of the September 11, 2001, attacks, and resolving the Arab-Israeli conflict, which indirectly fueled terrorism, violence, and extremism. President Obama believed that building

---

[29] Rhodes, B. The world as it is. Random House, The United States, New York, 2018 (p. 47).

bridges of understanding between the West, the United States, and Islam, especially in the Middle East and North Africa, was crucial. He viewed establishing democracy in the Arab world as an essential strategy to combat extremism and exclusion. Furthermore, he held a firm conviction that the rise of moderate Islam to power in the surrounding Arab countries could contribute to resolving religious conflicts, particularly the long-standing issue with Israel. Achieving this goal, he believed, would also have positive implications for limiting Muslim immigration to the West, potentially encouraging those who had left to return if conditions improved. Also, President Obama viewed the two-state solution, involving a halt to Israeli settlement construction and the principle of a land exchange between Israelis and Palestinians, as a just settlement to the costly Arab-Israeli conflict. In his approach, all religions were to preserve their rights to the Holy City of Jerusalem. This perspective aimed not only at regional stability but also at reducing the migration of Muslims to the West due to the historical persecution by existing regimes.

When President Obama addressed Arabs and Muslims from Egypt, he did so with a proactive and comprehensive Middle East initiative (project), not merely a speech. Rooted in the seven principles outlined in his New Beginning speech in Cairo, this approach aimed at confronting religious extremism and violence, resolving the Arab-Israeli conflict, addressing Iran's nuclear issue, preventing nuclear weapons proliferation, supporting change and democratization, advocating for religious freedoms and women's rights, and promoting economic development and job opportunities[30].

On August 12, 2010, President Obama penned a five-page confidential memo titled "Political Reform in the Middle East and North Africa (MENA)." The recipients included Vice President Joe Biden, Secretary of State Hillary Clinton, Secretary of Defense Robert Gates, National Security Adviser Tom Donilon, and other senior members of the foreign policy team. A study by Ryan Lizza in The New Yorker Magazine, published on May 11, 2011, delves into the contents of this memo. According to Lizza's analysis, President Obama expressed worry in the memo that efforts toward political reform and societal openness in the MENA were significantly declining, with potential halts in other regions. Even relatively liberal regimes in the area were tightening control over public gatherings, the press, freedom of expression, and activities of opposition political groups. The President noted a concerning trend: as popular discontent increased, ruling authorities in the region were more likely to resort to severe suppression rather than embracing reform. The memorandum reflected President Obama's vision and desire to balance political interests and high moral ideals.

---

[30] President Obama's Speech in Cairo: A New Beginning. The White House President Barack Obama Site. Retrieved from:

https://obamawhitehouse.archives.gov/blog/NewBeginning/transcripts.

Lizza's study concluded by highlighting a pivotal event: on December 17, 2010, Mohamed Bouazizi, a Tunisian vegetable seller, set himself on fire to protest political corruption. This incident ignited a series of revolutions across the region, reshaping the political landscape of the MENA.[31]

Why Did Obama's Middle East Approach Not Succeed?

President Obama's Middle East Approach was ambitious and distinguished itself from previous American attempts. Its comprehensive nature and Obama's earnest commitment set it apart. However, the initiative faced chronic challenges that led to its failure. Despite its notable features, multiple factors hindered its success. Firstly, the project was confronted by long-standing regional entitlements that had remained unresolved for over six decades since the conclusion of World War II in 1945. These historical complexities, deeply rooted in the region, posed formidable obstacles to Obama's initiatives. Furthermore, President Obama's Approach had to contend with new factors and developments stemming from the Arab Spring movement. The seismic shifts brought about by the Arab Spring introduced additional complexities and dynamics, further complicating the already intricate geopolitical landscape of the Middle East.

---

[31] The Consequentialist. A study by Rayan Lizza, Published in The New Yorker Magazine on May 11, 2011.

The failure of Obama's Middle East Initiative can be attributed to enduring historical issues and new challenges, particularly those triggered by the Arab Spring. The collision of these factors created a complex and challenging environment that proved difficult to navigate successfully. The following are among these factors:

1. The Syrian Revelation Tipped the Geopolitical Scale in the Middle East and Put President Obama's Global Leadership to the Test

The Syrian revolution, commencing in mid-March 2011, served as an early test for President Barack Obama's global crisis leadership, given Syria's geostrategic importance in the Middle East. Born out of the broader context of the Arab Spring uprisings, the Syrian revolution responded to a culmination of social and political grievances that had reached a boiling point, creating a profound sense of desperation, especially among the youth who endured the systemic challenges. The catalyst for this revolt was a pervasive atmosphere of unemployment, injustice, oppression, domination, tyranny, and humiliation that persisted throughout the rule of President Hafez al-Assad, who established the current regime in Syria through a military coup in 1970. Al-Assad sought to anchor his authority in the regional and international order by signing the Military Disengagement Agreement with Israel on May 31, 1974[32].

---

[32] On this day in 1974, Israel-Syria Military Disengagement Agreement was signed in Geneva. By JERUSALEM POST STAFF. The Jerusalem Post,

Following the 1973 War, Henry Kissinger, then U.S. Secretary of State, aimed to prevent more traditional wars between Arab nations and Israel like those that had happened before. His diplomatic efforts resulted in two key agreements, each with distinct outcomes. Firstly, unlike the military disengagement agreement with Syria, the peace treaty with Egypt in 1979 was a comprehensive resolution. It involved Israel returning all territories Egypt lost during the 1967 Six-Day War. Such a move effectively eliminated Egypt as a potential military threat to Israel. In contrast, the military disengagement agreement with Syria did not lead to a full peace treaty. It left unresolved issues, particularly regarding the Golan Heights, which Israel had occupied in 1967. This allowed for ambiguity, leaving the door open for potential Israeli expansion in Syria. Consequently, while Egypt was removed from the list of potential adversaries through a comprehensive peace treaty, Syria remained in a state of neither war nor peace with Israel for over four decades. The unresolved territorial disputes, exemplified by the retention of the Golan Heights, created a complex geopolitical landscape. The ramifications of these agreements were felt in the later years, notably during the Syrian revolution. The historical and geopolitical intricacies set the stage for challenges in the region, underscoring the significance of the diplomatic decisions made in the aftermath of the 1973 war. In his book, World Order, Henry released in 2015, Kissinger notes that: "In 1974, Syria and Israel successfully negotiated a disengagement

---

MAY 31, 2023, 11:49. Updated: MAY 31, 2023, 15:20. Retrieved from: https://www.jpost.com/israel-news/article-744687#google_ignette.

agreement. This accord aimed to delineate and safeguard the military lines of contact between the two nations. Remarkably, this agreement endured for four decades, withstanding various challenges, including conflicts against terrorism, and persisting through the intensification of the ongoing civil war in Syria"[33]. Kissinger's observation emphasizes the durability of regional arrangements despite changing geopolitical circumstances. Israel and Iran share a common interest in maintaining the stability of the Syrian regime, contradicting President Obama's New Middle East project that supported Arab Spring revolutions, including the Syrian revolution. Israel and Iran both have significant investments in the existing Syrian regime, making regime change unfavorable to their interests. President Obama's involvement in the Arab Spring revolutions included advocating for the removal of Egyptian President Hosni Mubarak, despite concerns from key national security team members, including Vice President Joe Biden, Secretary of State Hilary Clinton, and Secretary of Defense Robert Gates. The support for the election of President Mohmmad Morsi, associated with the Muslim Brotherhood, raised apprehensions for Israel, Iran, and the Syrian regime. This situation led to an unusual convergence of interests between other Arab governments, Israel, and Iran to suppress the Syrian revolution. This geopolitical shift, combined with Syria's strategic location and the post-U.S. occupation vacuum in Iraq, posed a

---

[33] Kissinger, H. World Order. Random House, New York. 2015. P. 116.

challenge to Obama's leadership, particularly in the context of the 2012 U.S. presidential election.

2. President Obama Faced a Stall Wall in Israel

During the escalating Syrian crisis, President Obama adopted a cautious approach to intervention, influenced significantly by Israeli pressure. Israel, led by Prime Minister Benjamin Netanyahu, preferred the stability of Bashar al-Assad's regime and was wary of potential alternatives. This stance contrasted with President Obama's strategy, not only regarding Syria but also in addressing the broader Arab-Israeli conflict. President Obama believed that resolving the Syrian crisis should be integrated into a comprehensive solution for the Middle East. Thus, he advocated a political solution that would force al-Assad to step down, leading to the formation of a transitional government under United Nations Resolution No. 2254. However, President Obama aimed to preserve the Syrian army, maintain the continuity of state institutions, and prevent their collapse to avoid a recurrence of the U.S. experience in Iraq. He argued that removing al-Assad from power could cut off Hezbollah Party's lifeline from Iran, potentially prompting the party to shift from a military to a political role, like other Lebanese parties. Additionally, he believed that persuading Israel to withdraw from the Lebanese-occupied territories, which Hezbollah used as a pretext for armed resistance, could contribute to this transformation. President Obama thought that al-Assad's fall and the neutralization of Hezbollah militarily could facilitate negotiations with Iran over its nuclear program. Such a situation, in turn, could yield results beneficial for both the United States and

Israel, preventing the need for military strikes and averting a costly regional war scenario that President Obama sought to avoid due to its contradictions with his aversion to warfare. President Obama believed that achieving tangible results in negotiations over the Iranian nuclear program would enable him to present an approach acceptable to Israel. He hoped that through negotiations with the Palestinians, he could realize his aspiration for peace in the Middle East before leaving the White House in January 2017.

President Obama's 2009 Nobel Peace Prize reception heightened the desire for success, underscoring expectations for diplomatic achievements. Therefore, President Obama purposefully sought a breakthrough in the Middle East crisis to secure his legacy as one of the great presidents, especially given his historic achievement as the first African American president. However, Prime Minister Netanyahu's stance disrupted his vision for the new Middle East. In his recent book, "A Promised Land," President Obama expressed his disappointment with the lack of progress toward peace in the Middle East. He also expressed his frustration with Israeli Prime Minister Benjamin Netanyahu's approach to the conflict, which he believed was not conducive to peace. Obama thought Netanyahu aimed to align U.S. policy in the Middle East with Israel's approach, which created a clash of visions and hindered Obama's pursuit of lasting peace in the region[34].

---

[34] Obama's Simmering Resentment of Benjamin Netanyahu. National Review. By Jim Geraghty, November 20, 2020, 6:30 AM. Published on:

3. Obama had to deal with Iran's Tactics and Deception.

On May 28, 2014, President Obama delivered a speech at the United States Military Academy in West Point, New York. In his remarks, he discussed the events in the Middle East, including the potential for an agreement with Iran on its nuclear program. He emphasized the need to collaborate with allies and partners, respect international law, and use diplomacy and development to address global challenges[35].

While he did not provide additional information, President Obama reiterated his commitment to avoiding military actions that would jeopardize American soldiers' lives. However, he took a nuanced stance, stating that he would not hesitate to use military force if the United States' security and interests were at risk. He did not elaborate on the specific dangers or interests warranting such action. The underlying message appeared directed at Iran, implying that the absence of an agreement on its nuclear program could directly threaten U.S. interests and security, potentially leading to the use of military force. President Obama aimed to set the stage for the upcoming 5+1 negotiations to finalize the Iran

---

https://www.nationalreview.com/2020/11/obamas-simmering-resentment-of-benjamin-netanyahu.

[35] Remarks by the President at the United States Military Academy Commencement Ceremony. U.S. Military Academy-West Point West Point, New York May 28, 2014. Published on the White House Site: Remarks by the President at the United States Military Academy Commencement Ceremony | whitehouse.gov (archives.gov)

nuclear agreement. He sought an agreement acceptable to Israel, hoping to convince the U.S. Congress not to renew sanctions against Iran in its July 20, 2014, session.

This move marked the last opportunity for Iran to engage in a deal with the United States and the West, and it was also President Obama's final chance to enhance his historical legacy. However, the agreement was not reached until the following year, on April 2, 2015, after Iran had secured economic and political gains, including the lifting of economic sanctions, the resumption of oil exports, particularly to China, and improved relations with Gulf Arab Countries, notably Saudi Arabia. Also, President Obama's shift to focus on combating ISIS, following the broader war on terrorism initiated by President George W. Bush, was perceived to benefit Iran. This change marked a transition from the post-9/11 war on "Islamic terrorism" to a more specific effort against ISIS and aspects of Sunni Islam. Furthermore, President Obama's reluctance to take decisive action in Syria is attributed to his desire for a deal with Iran, given the absence of a breakthrough with Israel.

4. President Obama's Pursuit of the Turkish Model for Moderate Islam of Governance Sparked Questions and Encountered Resistance

During the Arab Spring, President Obama looked to the Turkish Justice and Development Party (AKP) governance model, led by President Recep Tayyip Erdogan, to advocate for democratic change. However, critics raised concerns about the model's suitability for neighboring Arab countries. They pointed to

Turkey's secular history and long-standing democratic system as factors that might not align with the political contexts of the targeted countries[36].

Also, President Obama's reliance on Qatar for financial support during this transitional period led to various interventions, including support for the Islamic Resurgence Movement in Tunisia and the rise of the Muslim Brotherhood in Egypt, culminating in the election of Dr. Mohammad Morsi as the first civilian president since the 1952 revolution. These actions created tensions with Israel, which had a peace treaty with Egypt, and drew protests from Iran, a Shia state competing with Sunni states like Turkey. The move also alienated Saudi Arabia, which follows Wahhabism, unlike Qatar, which supported the Muslim Brotherhood Movement. Collectively, these countries, along with Russia, opposed President Obama's involvement in Syria, partly due to concerns about a competing Qatari gas pipeline reaching the Syrian port of Latakia on the Mediterranean[37].

---

[36] Seymen Atasoy. The Turkish Example: A Model for Change in the Middle East. Middle East Policy Council. Retrieved on December 20, 2023, from: The Turkish Example: A Model for Change in the Middle East? | Middle East Policy Council (mepc.org)

[37] Nafeez Ahmad. The US-Russian Gaz Pipeline in Syria may Destabilize Putin. Middle East Eye, October 3, 2015. Retrieved from: The US-Russia gas pipeline war in Syria could destabilize Putin | Middle East Eye

5. Other Challenges President Obama Faced

Also, President Obama encountered other challenges in implementing his New Middle East initiatives. One notable obstacle was his limited foreign policy experience upon assuming the presidency in 2009. Critics argue that his background was primarily in domestic issues, necessitating a rapid adaptation to the complexities of international relations[38].

Additionally, internal debates and differences of opinion within his administration further complicated matters, particularly in handling momentous events like the Arab Spring. The Arab Spring, marked by protests across the Middle East and North Africa, posed a complex challenge, with the administration divided over how to respond. This internal divergence reflected a broader debate on balancing support for democratic movements while maintaining regional stability.

The aftermath of the Iraq War, initiated by the previous administration under President George W. Bush, also cast a shadow on President Obama's Middle East endeavor. The withdrawal of U.S. troops and the resultant power vacuum contributed to ongoing

---

[38] Fawaz A Gerges. The Obama's approach to the Middle East: The End of American's Moment. international Affairs (Royal Institute of International Affairs 1944-). Vol. 89, No. 2 (March 2013), pp. 299-323 (25 pages). Published by Oxford University Press.

regional instability, requiring the Obama administration to navigate complex geopolitical dynamics.

President Obama's approach to foreign policy occasionally deviated from traditional American strategies, sparking debate and criticism. His pursuit of a more nuanced and diplomatic approach, sometimes seen as a departure from interventionist policies, garnered both support and opposition[39].

Obama's Middle East Approach: Obstacles

Summary and Conclusions

The most significant obstacles President Obama faced in realizing his goal for changes in the Middle East were Israeli intransigence in reaching a just and comprehensive settlement of the Palestinian cause and Iranian delays and tactics in agreeing on its nuclear program. This situation exacerbated the Syrian crisis due to the direct impact of both Iran and Israel on the conflict. Consequently, the settlement between Israelis and Palestinians, a focal point of President Obama's hope for the new Middle East, reached a standstill.

As a result, Obama's plans were disrupted, limiting his options and leading him to shift his focus from a seven-point project to a

---

[39] Based on a Commentary by Martin S. Indyk and Kenneth M Pollack. The Obama Administration: Facing Challenges in the Middle East. Brookings. January 13, 2010. Retrieved from: The Obama Administration: Facing Challenges in the Middle East | Brookings.

single point: the agreement with Iran on its nuclear program, the author metaphorically referred to as "Obama's Crown Jewel." This situation left other regional issues unresolved, and the emergence of ISIS further complicated the situation. In a study entitled, Why Obama failed in the Middle East from the Arab Spring to Syria, to Iran, to the Peace Process, and President Obama's actions did not reach the level of his lofty rhetoric, published in the Foreign Policy Magazine on April 2, 2013, Arron David Miller, a researcher at the Woodrow Wilson International Institute, stated that: "President Obama's legacy in the Middle East - an issue of concern to all U.S. presidents - lies in the hands of two of his staunchest foes: *Syrian President Bashar al-Assad and Iranian Supreme Leader Ali Khamenei. What makes matters worse and worries Obama is the third major player in this circle, with a notorious relationship with President Obama: Israeli Prime Minister Benjamin Netanyahu. The matter is harsh and complex because saving Syria, resolving the Iranian nuclear program, and achieving Israeli–Palestinian peace are matters beyond the President's ability, even if he boasts of the support of capable and dependable partners. The exciting thing is that Obama planned not to be a president who watches the disasters in the Middle East but rather one who transforms them for the better! And here he is now, the president, during whose reign the entire region poised to be in the worst condition ever.*

However, pressing questions remain in the minds of policymakers regarding U.S. President Barack Obama's policy toward the Middle East, specifically Iraq, Syria, and Iran. Among them, according to Miller: *Why did President Obama decide to abandon the Syrian revolution so early? Why does he seem more understanding of the Iranian position despite his admission that Iran supports terrorism? What is the explanation for his obsession with Sunni jihadists and his willingness to accept or overlook the role of Shiite jihadists against the Islamic State (ISIS)? Will the region pay the price for the personal ambitions of the American president[40]?"*

In 2007, before he started his presidential campaign, Barack Obama said, "My ambition is not to be on the list of presidents of the United States. My ambition is to be a president who makes something different." Journalist David Remnick, who interviewed Obama for the New Yorker, commented: "If George W. Bush's foreign policy is a reaction to September 11, then Obama's foreign policy is a reaction to a reaction." Miller also said, "Obama was fortunate, or unlucky, to be president in a historical period witnessing a transformation in the Middle East that occurs once in a century. Unless you face major events and can participate in shaping them. Miller cited, for example, Presidents Abraham Lincoln and Franklin Delano Roosevelt. Obama was fortunate enough to live up to the first part of this aphorism, his testimony of momentous events. Still, he could not, as his critics claim,

---

[40] Why Obama failed in the Middle East from the Arab Spring to Syria, to Iran, to the peace process, and President Obama's actions did not reach the level of his lofty rhetoric. A study by Arron David Miller, published in the Foreign Policy Magazine on April 2, 2013.

accomplish the second part of participating in shaping those events so history can remember him[41].

However, President Obama's administration confronted many intricate challenges in the Middle East, extending beyond the persistent Arab-Israeli conflict and the Iranian nuclear dilemma. Navigating this complex geopolitical landscape demanded a keen strategy to address regional intricacies and safeguard U.S. interests. Among these challenges were Turkey's evolving role under President Erdogan, Russian President Vladimir Putin's assertiveness in conflicts such as Syria, and China's Xi Jinping expanding China's influence in the Middle East through the Belt and Road Initiative (BRI). These nuanced geopolitical dynamics necessitated focused attention from the U.S., a consideration that subsequent administrations had to grapple with, as detailed in the following chapters.

---

[41] From an interview with Candidate Barack Obama by David Remnick, published in the New Yorker Magazine in 2007.

Chapter 3: The United States and Arab-Israeli Conflict

The Balfour Declaration was a significant historical event during World War I. In 1917, British Foreign Secretary Arthur James Balfour sent a letter to Lord Lionel Walter de Rothschild, a prominent figure in the Zionist movement, outlining British support for the establishment of a national home for the Jewish people in Palestine. The Balfour Declaration was the first step the Colonial West, particularly Great Britain, took toward creating a Jewish state in Palestine. The declaration, consisting of only sixty-seven words, is recognized for its profound impact on Middle Eastern and global history[42]. Part of the Balfour Declaration document is presented below.

---

[42]Balfour Declaration: The divisive legacy of sixty-seven words 1st November 2017, 08:04 EDT. By Yolande Knell, BBC News, Jerusalem. https://www.bbc.com/news/world-middle-east-41765892.

Foreign Office,
November 2nd, 1917.

Dear Lord Rothschild,

     I have much pleasure in conveying to you, on behalf of His Majesty's Government, the following declaration of sympathy with Jewish Zionist aspirations which has been submitted to, and approved by, the Cabinet

     His Majesty's Government view with favour the establishment in Palestine of a national home for the Jewish people, and will use their best endeavours to facilitate the achievement of this ...

Part of Balfour Declaration

Despite not explicitly mentioning the word "State," the Balfour letter expresses support for establishing a national home for the Jewish people in Palestine. However, the United States was the first country to officially recognize the newly established state of Israel in 1948. Nonetheless, his initial concern about the status of the other side, like President Roosevelt, President Harry Truman, was the first world leader to recognize Israel, making the acknowledgment only eleven minutes after Israel declared independence. Such a swift recognition played a significant role in establishing diplomatic relations between the United States and Israel. While President Franklin D. Roosevelt appeared sympathetic to the Jewish cause, his assurances to the Arabs that the United States would not intervene without consulting both parties caused public uncertainty about his position. When Harry S. Truman took office, he made clear that his sympathies were with the Jews and accepted the Balfour Declaration, explaining that it was in keeping with former President Woodrow Wilson's principle of self-determination[43].

The United Nations Resolution No. 181 stipulates partition and calls for the establishment of the State of Israel. The resolution was welcomed by Jews but opposed by Palestinians and Arabs, leading to their first war that lasted about a year. During this conflict, Israel, with British support, occupied lands that were initially designated for Palestinians, amounting to more than 20% of the natural area of Palestine. The original Palestinian inhabitants were expelled, and a new Jewish population from Europe and the United States replaced them. The war concluded with an armistice in 1949 between Israel and its neighboring Arab states, resulting in the West Bank being administered by Jordan and the Gaza Strip by Egypt. However, Israel occupied these territories and additional areas of Egypt, Syria, and Jordan in the 1967 war. Despite the Oslo Accords in 1993 advocating a two-state solution and Israel's unilateral withdrawal from the Gaza Strip in 2005, successive right-wing Israeli governments, particularly under Prime Minister Benjamin Netanyahu, continued to seize Palestinian land in the West Bank and East Jerusalem, constructing settlements despite

---

[43] Harry S. Truman and the Creation of Israel. Retrieved from: https://www.trumanlibrary.gov/museum/ordinary-man/recognition-of-israel.

objections from most American Presidents, except President Trump[44], as shown in Fig. 4 below.

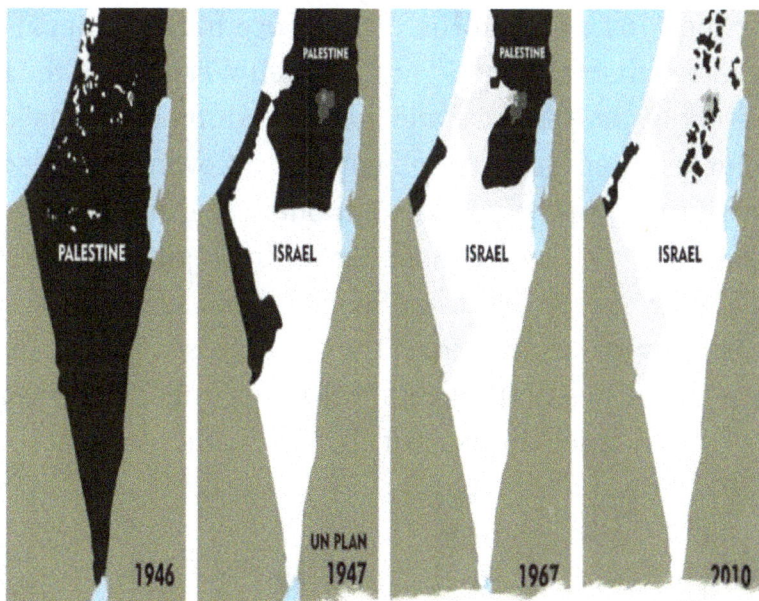

Figure No. 4 for a Map of Palestinian Loss of Land (1946-2010).

Figure 4: Palestinian Loss of Land (1946–2010)

---

[44] The 1967 Arab Israeli War. The Department of State. Historian Office. Retrieved from: https://history.state.gov/milestones/1961-1968/arab-israeli-war-1967.

The U.S. and Paths of War and Peace in the Middle East after 1967

After the 1967 war, the Historian Office in the Department of State reported that: "The 1967 Arab-Israeli War marked the failure of the Eisenhower, Kennedy, and Johnson administrations' efforts to prevent renewed Arab-Israeli conflict following the 1956 Suez War. Unwilling to return to what National Security Advisor Walter Rostow called the "tenuous chewing gum and string arrangements" established after Suez, the Johnson administration sought Israel's withdrawal from the territories it had occupied in exchange for peace settlements with its Arab neighbors. This formula has remained the basis of all U.S. Middle East peacemaking efforts."[45]

After President Richard Nixon's inauguration in January 1969, he directed his Secretary of State, William Rogers, to initiate a peace effort between the Arab nations and Israel based on United Nations Security Council Resolution No. 242. This resolution advocated the "land in exchange for peace" principle, commonly known as Land for Peace, calling for Israel to withdraw from the territories it occupied during the 1967 war. However, Israel interpreted the resolution in its own way, asserting that it was obligated to withdraw only from the specific lands it had occupied, not from all territories. Dr. Kameel Naufal, President Nixon's official interpreter, wrote: "Upon the death of Egyptian President

---

[45]The Historian Office. https://history.state.gov/milestones/1961-1968/arab-israeli-war-1967

Gamal Abdel Nasser in September 1970, Mr. Anwar Al-Sadat succeeded him. Al-Sadat secretly contacted President Nixon immediately after Nasser's funeral through a letter'""[46]. The content of the letter was kept secret, as Dr. Naufal stated. However, in 1973, President Sadat later expressed Egypt's openness to peace with Israel. Sadat's condition for peace was the return of territories, including the Sinai Peninsula, occupied by Israel during the 1967 Six-Day War. But Israeli Prime Minister Golda Meir responded, asserting to Henry Kissinger, Secretary of State, that Egypt, having lost the 1967 war, could not dictate terms but instead should accept them[47].

Dissatisfied with Meir's stance and aiming for a comprehensive peace process, Kissinger opted for a different strategy. When Sadat sought Kissinger's opinion, the U.S. Secretary of State suggested that Israel might not be inclined to accept peace in a position of strength and triumphant ecstasy, deeming it potentially hazardous. Subsequently, President Sadat secretly collaborated with Syrian President Hafez al-Assad to launch a sudden war against Israel. Coordination efforts also involved consultations with King Hussein of Jordan. Despite initial doubts and speculations, the Yom Kippur War unfolded on October 6, 1973.

---

[46] Naufal, K. "Arab America Misrule Hostages." Dar A Nahar for Publication, Beirut, Lebanon, 2003, p.191.

[47] When Golda Meir Pulled the Impossible. By Uri Kaufman. Hadassah Magazine, September 2023. Retrieved from: When Golda Meir Pulled Off the Impossible | Hadassah Magazine.

Widespread belief in the Arab world holds that Secretary Kissinger orchestrated the war to establish new conditions for advancing the stalled peace process. However, the statement notes a lack of credible sources to substantiate this claim, highlighting the complexity of historical events and the multiple perspectives surrounding them.

During the October War in 1973, the Egyptian army successfully crossed the Suez Canal and destroyed the well-known Bar-Lev Defensive Line. This accomplishment by Egypt led to the recovery of part of the Sinai Peninsula. Simultaneously, Syria liberated a portion of its occupied lands. Unexpectedly, King Faisal of Saudi Arabia approved an oil embargo on the United States and countries supporting Israel in the war[48]. As the conflict evolved into a war of attrition, it persisted until direct American intervention. The United Nations Security Council responded by issuing Resolution No. 338, which immediately halted all military actions and initiated talks between the warring parties under UN auspices, followed by Resolutions No. 339 and 340. Then, a disengagement agreement between Israel and Egypt, signed on **January 18, 1974,** provided for Israeli withdrawal to the west of Sinai, while Egypt was to reduce

---

[48] The Yom Kippur of 1973 War. Surprise Attacks from Egypt and Syria had Israel fight for survival. By Robert McNamara. Updated on February 21, 2020. Retrieved from: The Yom Kippur War of 1973 (thoughtco.com/

the size of its forces on the east bank of the canal. A similar agreement was signed between Israel and Syria on May 31, 1974[49].

Subsequently, Egyptian President Anwar al-Sadat took a historic step by signing the Camp David Peace Treaty with Israel Prime Minister Menachem Begin in 1979 under the leadership of U.S. President Jimmy Carter. President Carter's decision to establish the American Rapid Intervention Forces in 1977 was noteworthy, specifically aimed at protecting the oil wells in Saudi Arabia and the Gulf States. This move was motivated by the fear of the recurrence of the oil embargo imposed by King Faisal, who was assassinated in March 1975. The Camp David Peace Treaty marked a significant diplomatic breakthrough in the region, solidifying peace between Egypt and Israel with the support of the United States[50].

Madrid Peace Conference and Oslo Accords

After the conclusion of the U.S.-led war on Iraq following the invasion of Kuwait, President George H.W. Bush instructed his Secretary of State, James Baker, to organize an international conference in Madrid, Spain. The conference, held from October 30

---

[49] Israel-Egypt Disengagement Agreement (1974). ECF.ORG, Issue 179. Retrieved from: ECF - Economic Cooperation Foundation: Israel-Egypt Disengagement Agreement (1974.)

[50] September 7, 1978, Camp David Accord Signed. Retrieved form the History Site: Camp David Accords signed | September 17, 1978, | HISTORY.

to November 1, 1991, aimed to address the long-standing Arab-Israeli conflict[51].

This diplomatic initiative laid the groundwork for subsequent secret negotiations between Israelis and Palestinians in Oslo, Norway. Shimon Peres, then the Foreign Affairs Minister, represented the Israeli side in these clandestine talks. On the Palestinian side, Mahmoud Abbas, the head of the Foreign Affairs Department of the Palestine Liberation Organization (PLO), took a leading role. The Oslo Accords, the result of these negotiations, marked a significant development in the ongoing peace process between Israel and Palestine. In September 1993, then-Israeli Prime Minister Yitzhak Rabin and the head of the Palestine Liberation Organization (PLO), Yasser Arafat, signed the Declaration of Principles under the auspices of U.S. President Bill Clinton. This agreement outlined the principles of a future peace process, aiming to establish an interim self-rule authority in the Palestinian territories for five years to move towards a two-state solution. In May of the same year, the first part of the agreement was implemented, with Arafat entering Gaza for the first time, and international aid commenced for the Palestinian National Authority (PNA). However, "Rabin was assassinated on November 4, 1995, by Yigal Amir, an extremist Jew who was opposed to the

---

[51] The 1991 Madrid Peace Conference. Association for Diplomatic Studies and Training (ADST), October 15, 2015. Retrieved from: The 1991 Madrid Peace Conference – Association for Diplomatic Studies & Training (adst.org).

Oslo Accords and the handing over of control of portions of the West Bank to the Palestinians as part of the landmark agreement"[52].

In 1998, Palestinian Authority President Yasser Arafat and Israeli Prime Minister Benjamin Netanyahu signed the Wye River Agreement near Washington, D.C. Subsequently, the Likud Government, led by Netanyahu, fell, and the Labor government, headed by Ehud Barak, took over. In 2000, during the Camp David meeting, Mr. Barak presented a proposal to Mr. Arafat for establishing a Palestinian State in the entire Gaza Strip and certain parts of the West Bank, with East Jerusalem as its capital. President Bill Clinton sponsored this meeting before leaving the White House in 2001. Despite the significant proposal, Mr. Arafat categorically rejected it, as he found it challenging to garner support for the plan among the Palestinian people. This rejection played a role in the subsequent complexities and challenges in the Israeli-Palestinian peace process[53].

---

[52] Ex-Shin Bet accuses Netanyahu of lying about lead-up to Rabin assassination. The Time of Israel. July 3, 2023, 1:27 pm.

[53] Inci Sakyi. Timeline: How the Israeli-Palestinian Peace Process Fell Apart in the Three Decades After the 1993 Oslo Accords. Frontline, November 7, 2023. Retrieved from: Timeline: How the Israeli-Palestinian Peace Process Fell Apart in the Three Decades After the 1993 Oslo Accord | FRONTLINE (pbs.org).

RIAD S. AISAMI

The Two-State Solution is Dead

In an article titled "The Two-State Solution: What It Is and Why It Has Not Happened?" Published in the New York Times on December 29, 2016, Max Fisher discussed the concept of the two-state solution, which envisions the establishment of an independent Palestinian state alongside Israel. The idea is that this arrangement would address Israel's security concerns, allowing it to maintain a Jewish demographic majority (preserving the country's Jewish and democratic character) while also providing the Palestinians with their state. Most governments and international bodies, including the United States, officially support the two-state solution, which has been a central goal of peace talks for decades. Despite widespread support, Fisher highlighted four challenging factors that have made the two-state solution difficult to achieve: borders, Jerusalem, refugees, and security. These issues have been significant points of contention in negotiations between Israel and the Palestinians. Fisher also noted skepticism regarding the viability of the two-state solution, with others arguing that it is effectively dead. One reason cited for this skepticism is the actions of Israeli Prime Minister Benjamin Netanyahu, who, despite endorsing the two-state solution in a speech in 2009, continued to expand West Bank settlements. Furthermore, in 2015, Mr. Netanyahu stated that there would be no withdrawals or concessions, casting doubt on his commitment to a two-state resolution under his leadership. This skepticism has fueled debates about the future of the Israeli-Palestinian peace process and the prospects for achieving a two-state solution[54].

The continuous expansion of Israeli settlements in the West Bank has exacerbated this impasse. As a result, the maximum concessions that even the most accommodating Israelis are willing to make regarding the historic land of Palestine fall significantly short of the minimum requirements acceptable to the most conciliatory Palestinians, hindering the establishment of a viable Palestinian state.

President Trump's Deal of The Century Proposal

On January 28, 2019, President Donald Trump held a press conference at the White House to announce what he termed the "Deal of the Century" for peace in the Middle East. "Standing alongside him was Benjamin Netanyahu, the prime minister of the Israeli caretaker government at the time. The announcement's timing coincided with both leaders facing legal challenges, with corruption and abuse of power trials underway for Trump and Netanyahu[55]. During the press conference, President Trump

---

[54] What It Is and Why It Has Not Happened. An article by Max Fisher, published in the New York Times on December 29, 2016.

[55] Netanyahu and Trump: Two desperate men exploiting power to save themselves. By Chris McGrail in New York. The Guardian. Published on: Netanyahu and Trump: two desperate men exploiting power to save themselves | Israel | The Guardian.

provided limited details about the deal. However, Mr. Trump emphasized the deal's greatness and described it as the last chance for peace in the Middle East. President Trump highlighted the plan's key elements for the Palestinians, stating that in exchange for agreeing to the deal, they would receive a "state" in "some areas" of the West Bank, along with Gaza, connected by a corridor. The capital of this Palestinian state would be located somewhere in East Jerusalem. President Trump also stated that wealthy countries would contribute $50 billion in economic aid to the Palestinians. He anticipated Palestinian rejection initially but suggested that economic conditions would eventually compel their acceptance. He gave the Palestinians four years to consider the proposal. Prime Minister Netanyahu then took the floor, detailed, refuted, and confirmed various provisions of the plan, particularly those benefiting Israel. He stressed that Israel should be recognized as a Jewish state with a united Jerusalem as its capital. The plan included sovereignty over Jewish settlements in the West Bank, control along the borders west of the Jordan River, security control over the Jordan Valley, and the potential acquisition of an area north of the Dead Sea. Mr. Netanyahu also emphasized maintaining control over the Golan Heights, which had been annexed by Israel in 1981. In expressing his gratitude, Mr. Netanyahu referred to President Trump as a "great man" who would go down in history as a peacemaker and stabilizer in the Middle East. However, the joint announcement sparked mixed reactions globally, with some supporting and others criticizing the proposed plan. The complete plan is 181 pages and contains twenty-two sections covering a range of issues, including the legitimate aspirations of both sides, the two-state solution, the status of Jerusalem, sovereignty, borders, security, refugees, detainees, border crossings, the Gaza Strip, and commercial exchange. In economic matters, it promises international investment of more than $50 billion over 10 years as part of a regional economic integration program. It also has four annexes: one on the proposed borders for the two states; one on Israel's security concerns, particularly its total control over the Jordan Valley; one on the counter-terror criteria that the Palestinian state should meet; and one consolidating Israeli security control over a 'disarmed' Palestinian state, including the right to directly intervene in any potential threats it sees within the latter's borders. Finally, it confirms international crossings with Jordan and Egypt and regulates the territorial waters of the proposed Palestinian state[56].

The Trump Administration is hawking the same solution suggested by the Israeli extreme years ago. Having made some minor modifications and benefiting from Palestinian and Arab divisions, and the failure of the Palestinian leadership to produce any clear strategy to combat a project that has already primarily been implemented on the ground throughout the last few years, Trump is presenting it as a novel American proposal. However, while the circumstances may seem favorable in the United States and Israel for its implementation, the plan is unlikely to win

---

[56] The Manama Workshop: Trump's Middle East Peace Plan Plummets before Lift-Off," Situation Assessment, ACRPS, 01/07/2019 (accessed on 03/02/2020 at https://bit.ly/2RUcoE7.)

widespread Palestinian approval and most assuredly will not be given any legitimacy[57].

Israel and the Jewish State Quest

Overall, Israel has never been interested in the two-state solution, and Israel's quest to be a unilateral Jewish state has become undeniable. It aims to extend over the entire territory of "religious Israel," which is the same natural borders of Palestine, extending from the Mediterranean Sea to the Jordan River. Benjamin Netanyahu, the Prime Minister of Israel, drew the "lines on the sand" at the last time the United States called on the parties, the Israeli Government, and the Palestinian Authority to return to talks. He said: *"We desire the return of negotiations with the Palestinians with no conditions if these negotiations guarantee Israel the unilateral Jewish state and complete control over Jerusalem, and not to go back to the borders of June 4, 1967, and the retention of the large settlements in the West Bank. And they are guaranteeing the right of the Israeli army to deploy east of the Jordan River. This move is to protect the security of Israel for fear of the inability of the expected Palestinian state, because of the negotiations, to protect it[58].*

---

[57] Deal of the Century: What is and Why Now? Arab Center for Research and Policy Studies (ACRPS). Arab Center in Washington DC. February 4, 2020.

[58] Based on a letter that sent from Prime Minister of Israel Netanyahu to Mr. John Kerry, then the Secretary of State, to express Israel's interest to

The conditions outlined by Mr. Netanyahu were not intended as a starting point for negotiations with the Palestinians but rather as a roadmap toward a unilateral solution imposed in advance. This same approach, which put the American sponsor in a challenge with then-Secretary of State John Kerry, was interpreted as a call to end negotiations before they even began, highlighting the US's crucial role in the peace process.

To establish a Jewish state in the Middle East, Israel is described as dealing with three fundamental pillars: **borders, population, and incubator**. In terms of borders, Israel's construction of the separation wall, cutting into parts of the West Bank and applying to East Jerusalem, is noted as a factor influencing the definition of its initial borders. The expansion of Israel's current area within the West Bank is portrayed as bringing it closer to the desired borders of a Jewish state. However, this expansion could limit the available land for a viable and survivable Palestinian state. Additionally, Mr. Netanyahu took steps to separate the fate of the West Bank from the Gaza Strip. Hence, the repeated wars in Gaza are seen as a designed effort to disconnect the negotiation tracks of the West Bank and Gaza and undermine the principle of the two-state solution, as outlined in the Oslo Accords. This reintroduces the confederation project between the West Bank and Jordan and between Gaza and Sinai in Egypt. This approach aligns with what

---

resume the peace talk with the Palestinian Authority without pre-conditions, as he stated.

the "deal of the century" presented by former President Trump aimed to achieve, connecting with Israel's pursuit of a Jewish state. Also, Israel's focus on its population as a crucial pillar consistently stipulates that Palestinian refugees will not be able to return to the 1948 Area. Thus, the refusal to release Palestinian prisoners from Jerusalem or the 1948 area is a non-negotiable issue for Israel. Also, the Israeli government is accused of systematically sponsoring decisions that would harass residents in these areas, potentially forcing them to leave. This is illustrated by the efforts to forcibly displace Bedouins from the Negev Desert and demolish their villages[59]. The third pillar for establishing and maintaining the Jewish State focuses on creating an incubator in the surrounding region by establishing similar states and religious/ethnic entities. The idea is that having entities around Israel with similar characteristics justifies its existence as another religious entity in the region and enhances its continuity. The presence of neighboring entities is portrayed to keep them preoccupied with internal conflicts, diverting their attention away from Israel. Examples of this strategy are highlighted in the ongoing conflicts in Syria, Iraq, and Lebanon, marked by sectarian strife along Shiite-Sunni lines. These conflicts aim to establish entities where each party (Sunni and Shiite) represents the

---

[59] Israel's apartheid against Palestinians: a cruel system of domination and a crime against humanity. Amnesty International, February 1, 2022. Retrieved from: Israel's apartheid against Palestinians: a cruel system of domination and a crime against humanity - Amnesty International

majority[60]. However, sectarian strife is a contagious and deadly epidemic, and the divisions on sectarian or ethnic grounds cannot simply be drawn on maps but require years of conflict. Additionally, religious states like empires face challenges. They may collapse due to expansion beyond their borders, as seen with historical examples like the Islamic State, the Ottoman Empire, and the Persian Empire. Also, potential challenges within a Jewish State may include discontent among various ethnic and religious groups, such as Ethiopian Jews, African Jews, Jews of Arab and Eastern origins, and Russian Jews. These challenges can be potential sources of internal tension that could impact the stability of the state. Israel's approach challenges the logic of natural survival. Instead of adapting to its environment, it attempts to reshape that environment to align with its unrealistic ambitions. According to Darwinian principles, survival belongs to those who can adapt more effectively. According to Darwinian Logic, life is for those who can adapt better.

The U.S. and Arab-Israeli Conflict

"Summary, Conclusions, and Recommendations"

Seventy-five years have passed since the establishment of Israel in 1948. In this time span, Israel, with the support of the United States, has engaged in five wars with Arab nations and participated in six conflicts involving Gaza following its

---

[60] Israel borders explained in maps. BBC, 11th October 2023, 6:56 EDT. Retrieved from: Israel's borders explained in maps (bbc.com).

withdrawal from the territory in 2005. Despite the passage of thirty years since the Oslo Accords in 1993, sponsored by the U.S., which endorsed a two-state solution, a resolution to the Israeli-Palestinian conflict remains elusive. The current trajectory of Israeli policies, particularly those led by the right-wing government under Prime Minister Benjamin Netanyahu, poses significant challenges to the viability of the two-state solution. The persistence of settlement construction, combined with the limited number of Jews globally and their inability to dominate the surrounding Arab and Muslim populations, makes the establishment of a Unilateral Jewish State unrealistic. Solutions imposed on the Palestinian people by force to accept any deal, such as President Trump's "deal of the century," may create difficult circumstances for the Palestinians, but are unlikely to uproot them from their land in Palestine. Also, the internal heterogeneity among Jews in Israel, including differences between Eastern and Western Jews, Ashkenazim, and Jews from various regions, could become a source of division in the absence of external conflict. Besides, the continuous fear of war and instability leads to a reversal of immigration, further highlighting the impracticality of such a belief. Statistics have found that increased Jews are leaving Israel despite the government's attempts to increase their numbers. Reverse migration has been a sensitive issue for Israel throughout the years, with the government offering money, housing, jobs, and what they advertise to be a better quality of life to Jews who choose to live in the country. Following the passing of the Nation-State Law in 2016, which set into law that Israel is the nation-state of all Jews and officially classed Arab citizens as second-class, Israel has increased its calls for Jews to immigrate. Each year, thousands of Jews move to Israel from Europe, the U.S.,

Russia, and around the world with the promise of a better quality of life. They move to illegal settlements in the West Bank, where they reap government rewards, including amenities, housing, education, and health care paid for by the state. However, figures released by the Midgame Research Institute, following research conducted in 2017, revealed that 27 percent of the Jewish population in Israel would leave the country if they could. The main reasons for the people's urge to leave the country were a lack of security, a challenging economic situation, and harsh living conditions[61].

The demographic challenge facing Israel is a critical factor, with projections suggesting that the Arab population in and around Palestine could outnumber the Jewish population in Israel three to four times in the future. Drawing parallels with the experience of South Africa, demographic imbalances could play a significant role in shaping Israel's future. According to a report by The Hill, the Jewish population in Israel accounts for 37.7% of the total population. In contrast, the State of Palestine population is estimated to be slightly more than half the size of Israel's. The same report suggests that the Jewish population of the combined

_____

[61] Reverse migration: The hidden reasons behind Jews leaving Palestine. July 3, 2019. Published in Israel Middle East News.

population is projected to decline to 46% by 2030 and 40 to 45% by 2048[62].

Furthermore, reverse immigration from Israel is expected to increase significantly following the recent attack by Hamas on Israel **on October 7, 2023**, and the ongoing massive conflict in Gaza. The instability in the region and the lack of security for both Palestinians and Israelis contribute to heightened vulnerability, potentially leading to a rise in immigration from Israel. Considering the changing global landscape, marked by economic integration and common interests among neighboring countries, it becomes imperative for both Arabs and Jews in Palestine to seek common ground and shared interests for coexistence in peace. Besides, the sustainability of normalization efforts with Arab countries may be influenced by Israel's current policies of domination and alienation. However, lessons from the experiences of Egypt and Jordan indicate that normalization with other Arab countries may not necessarily lead to the desired outcomes for Israel over time. The United States has long tried to negotiate a resolution to the Israeli-Palestinian conflict. Still, several factors, including deep divisions between and within the parties and declining U.S. interest in conducting traditional honest broker roles, have hurt the chances of a peace deal[63]. Maintaining the

---

[62] The demographic challenges to peace for Israel and Palestine. By Joseph Chamie. The Hill, October 20, 2022. Retrieved from: The demographic challenges to peace for Israel and Palestine | The Hill

[63] What Is U.S. Policy on the Israel- Palestinian Conflict? Backgrounder. written by Keli Robinson. Council on Foreign Relations. Published on:

current status quo in the Israeli-Palestinian conflict is not a viable option. The situation will escalate over time, causing further regional instability and global repercussions. Thus, it is imperative to seek a comprehensive and enduring resolution, considering the legitimate concerns of both the Palestinian and Israeli populations. Active and constructive engagement by the United States is crucial for achieving a sustainable solution. The establishment of Israel is closely tied to the support it receives from the United States, making its connection significant in the Middle East. However, this mutual dependence should not continue. The United States, being a key player in the region, must be impartial and take responsibility for finding solutions to this problem rather than exacerbating contemporary issues. Israel is often seen as the last remaining occupying state in history. To address the root issue, it is essential to reconsider the unconditional and extensive support from the United States and take steps toward ending the occupation. So, the United States can address other issues in the region, such as the Iranian nuclear program and influence, and the Syrian conflict, as discussed in subsequent chapters.

---

https://www.cfr.org/backgrounder/what-us-policy-israeli-palestinian-conflict. Last updated July 12, 2023.

Chapter 4: The United States and Iran's Nuclear Program and Its Influence in the Region

The history of the Iranian nuclear program is rooted in the mid-fifties of the last century, during the reign of Shah Mohammad Reza Pahlavi (1941-1979). The Shah aspired to make Iran a regional superpower, and his ambitions for nuclear capabilities began over two decades before the Mullahs' regime, following the Islamic Revolution in 1979[64]. During this period, the Shah fostered strong ties with the West, particularly the United States, which provided direct support since World War II. This support was strategic, as the U.S. sought allies in its Cold War conflict with the Soviet Union and aimed to control oil production in the Middle East. The U.S. played a pivotal role in overthrowing the government of Muhammad Mossadegh in 1953, solidifying the Shah's rule, and establishing a strategic partnership with Iran. The U.S.-Iran cooperation peaked

---

[64] Sina Azodi. A history of continuity in Iran's long nuclear program. Atlantic Council, December 8, 2020. Retrieved from: A history of continuity in Iran's long nuclear program - Atlantic Council.

after Iran joined the Baghdad Pact in 1955 with U.S. backing, assuming the role of the region's "Policeman" or Gulf Policeman[65].

In 1957, the U.S. and Iran signed their first nuclear cooperation agreement for peaceful and civilian purposes, lasting ten years. This agreement facilitated Iran's access to atomic aid, technical ability, and limited amounts of enriched uranium for research purposes. The collaboration also established the first nuclear research center at the University of Tehran in 1959[66].

In a recent study titled 'The Iranian Nuclear Program: Origins and Development,' issued by the Egyptian Institute for Studies and published in April 2022, researcher Omar Al-Sheik provides a historical background for the evolution of Iran's Nuclear Program as follows:

---

[65] SHREEYA SINHA and SUSAN CAMPBELL BEACHY. Timeline on Iran Nuclear Program. New York Times, April 2, 2015. Retrieved from: Timeline on Iran's Nuclear Program - The New York Times (nytimes.com/

[66] Major milestones of Iran's nuclear program Since 1957, the United States played a crucial role in the establishment of Iran's nuclear program. By Ted Regencia and Alia Chughtai. Published by Aljazeera on 5 Nov 20185 Nov 2018: https://www.aljazeera.com/news/2018/11/5/major-milestones-of-irans-nuclear-programme#:~:text=Eisenhower%20in%201953.-,1959,the%20Tehran%20Nuclear%20Research%20Center.

"*Iran purchased a nuclear research reactor from the United States, enhancing its nuclear capabilities. With German assistance, Iran began building a nuclear power reactor in Bushehr. Despite the promising strategic cooperation, internal disputes arose within the United States regarding this approach. In 1969, the U.S.-Iranian agreement for cooperation in peaceful atomic energy was renewed, extending for another decade. The seventies witnessed considerable progress in Iranian nuclear activities, supported by the U.S. The Shah established the Iranian Atomic Energy Organization in 1974, and agreements with the U.S., Germany, and France followed, allowing Iran to acquire the technology necessary for enrichment and a share of enriched uranium. So, the historical roots of the Iranian nuclear program trace back to the mid-fifties, marked by the Shah's ambitions, strong U.S.-Iran strategic cooperation, and significant developments in atomic activities during the seventies.*

After the Islamic Revolution in 1979, Iran's nuclear program shifted focus. It was initially halted due to religious leaders' opposition. However, the program resumed in the mid-1980s. Motivated by Iraq's use of weapons of mass destruction during the Iran-Iraq War, Iran sought to develop a nuclear deterrent. Despite setbacks, it established new research centers, cooperated with France and Pakistan, and invested in advanced security systems. In the early 1990s, Iran recruited Russian scientists and sought assistance from China and North Korea. While denying the intent to build nuclear weapons, Iran actively pursued nuclear capabilities, marking a significant shift in its strategic goals. In 1996, Russia announced the completion of the Bushehr reactor construction in 55 months, following a 1995 agreement. Despite U.S. pressure, Iran and Russia signed a contract for six 1000-megawatt electric and atomic stations. In July 2000, Russia expressed willingness to build five more nuclear reactors in Iran, outlining expanded cooperation until 2012, covering nuclear, economic, and military aspects. Since 2012, Iran's atomic activities have persisted despite assurances of peaceful intent. U.S. politicians allege hidden military motives, leveraging the issue for domestic support, especially during elections. Iran strategically imposes negotiation conditions, leveraging its nuclear capabilities for regional leadership. It takes advantage of global changes and seeks a nuclear deterrent due to neighboring nuclear states, the U.S. presence, and Israel's concerns. Despite increasing sanctions, Iran resists U.S. and EU demands to halt its nuclear program, anticipating potential regime change attempts. The U.S. and EU aim to prevent Iran from acquiring nuclear weapons, but Iran doubts their sincerity. The belief that the U.S. invaded Iraq on false premises strengthens Iran's resolve, seeing it as beneficial for its regional influence"[67].

Since 2003, after the United States occupied Iraq, Iran has become a major geopolitical force due to the vacuum left by Iraq and later Syria. Also, Iran strategically controls Hezbollah in Lebanon, shaping decision-making processes. The U.S.-induced destruction of Iraq in the 1990s boosted Iran's military capabilities. The neglect of Iran's influence during nuclear negotiations under President Obama increased its regional sway. Iran's control of

---

[67] Iranian Nuclear Program: The Iranian Nuclear Program: Origins and Development. A study by Omar Al-Sheikh. Issued by the Egyptian Institute for Studies. Published in April 2022 on www.eipss-eg.org.

Yemen by the Houthis and defiance against perceived U.S. bias resonates across Arab and Muslim populations. U.S. sanctions, especially under President Trump, prompted Iranians to resist perceived arrogance and biased treatment. The acquisition of nuclear capabilities by Iran could trigger regional nuclear competition involving Saudi Arabia, Turkey, and Egypt. The U.S. may struggle to prevent Iran from becoming a nuclear state, considering Israel's atomic arsenal. Addressing the nuclear crisis should involve all global and regional nuclear states, not just focusing on Israel and Iran[68].

Iran Benefitting from the Marginalization of Iraq

After 44 years of the Islamic Revolution, Iran's nuclear ambitions threaten Israel and challenge U.S. dominance in the region. President George W. Bush's Iraq policies inadvertently strengthened Iran's influence in Iraq. Also, the U.S. withdrawal from Iraq in 2011 by President Obama lacked a clear strategy, contributing to the persisting confusion in Syria. The absence of a coherent U.S. vision for the Middle East allows Iran to advance its nuclear program and complicates the regional dynamics. The U.S. occupation of Iraq, marked by the fall of Saddam Hussein's regime, is widely viewed as a strategic mistake that created a geopolitical

---

[68] Robert Einhorn and Richard Nephew. The Iran Nuclear Deal: Prelude to Proliferation in the Middle East. Brookings, May 31, 2016. Retrieved from: The Iran nuclear deal: Prelude to proliferation in the Middle East? | Brookings

vacuum in the Middle East. Disbanding the Iraqi army and overthrowing state institutions weakened Iraq, allowing Iran to extend its influence in political, economic, and human capacities. Also, the U.S. prioritizing Israel's security over regional stability further facilitated Iran's expansion. However, the convergence of interests between Iran and Israel in supporting the Syrian regime, despite differing goals, remained stable for years. Both benefited from conflicting religious and sectarian entities on their borders.

As Iran neared obtaining nuclear capabilities, concerns about a nuclear-armed Iran led to considerations of military action, with Israel contemplating an attack on Iran's nuclear facilities. However, in 2014, President Obama, prioritizing negotiations and rejecting preemptive wars, resisted Israeli pressure for military intervention. The potential financial cost of war with Iran, estimated at $2 trillion, and the strategic challenges made military action less feasible for the United States. A simulation study suggested that even a conventional Israeli strike might only delay Iran's nuclear program for a limited time, emphasizing the complexity of the situation[69]. Also, President Obama, motivated by

---

[69] Middle East Memo Number 21 October 2012. A SERIES OF UNFORTUNATE EVENTS: A CRISIS SIMULATION OF A U.S.-IRANIAN CONFRONTATION KENNETH M. POLLACK.

https://www.brookings.edu/wp-content/uploads/2016/06/us-iran-crisis-simulation-pollack-paper.pdf.

his Nobel Peace Prize and strategic considerations, resisted war for any reason other than a direct threat to U.S. national security.

He pursued negotiations to prevent Iran from acquiring nuclear weapons, overlooking other regional issues. The Joint Comprehensive Plan of Action (JCPOA) aimed at this goal, emphasizing Iran's involvement in the international market. However, President Trump, upon taking office in 2017, withdrew from the JCPOA, fulfilling a campaign promise. He imposed stricter sanctions on Iran, raising questions about the U.S.'s ability to activate the unilateral withdrawal mechanism outlined in the agreement's Articles 36 and 37. Legal experts argue that explicit withdrawal prevents the U.S. from utilizing the agreement's dispute settlement mechanisms. President Trump's executive order solidified the withdrawal, leaving the JCPOA's future uncertain[70].

In 2018, President Trump formally pulled out of the Nuclear Agreement that President Obama's administration signed with Iran in 2015—in an opinion on U.S. Foreign Policy published in The Guardian, Senator Bernie Sanders warned that by ending the Iran deal, Trump put America on the path to war. He also stated that we need to talk with Iran's government, seek a better relationship with

---

[70] Scenarios of the diplomatic conflict regarding the nuclear agreement with Iran and the activation of the "trigger finger." Mahmoud Al-Bazzi. A study issued by Al Jazeera Center for Studies on August 26, 2020.

the Iranian people, and a more constructive role for Iran in the region[71].

Thomas Friedman wrote in an opinion page in the New York Times: *"It turns out that Trump and Pompeo overplayed their hand. Had they been savvy, they would have told the Iranians that the U.S. would restore the deal and lift sanctions if Iran would agree to forgo enrichment to levels needed for a nuclear weapon for, say, 25 years — rather than the original 15 years. (I would have applauded that.) But, instead, they demanded changes in Iran's behavior so sweeping that the regime understood that the sanctions would never end"*[72].

Upon assuming the presidency in 2021, President Biden aimed to revive the 2015 Iran nuclear deal. However, negotiations have hit a roadblock as Iran insists on a narrow focus limited to the nuclear program. Emerging global variables, like Russia's war on Ukraine, necessitate a reevaluation of negotiation objectives. Yet, Iran exhibits no sign of altering its negotiation stance, leaving the fate of the agreement uncertain, hovering between implementation

---

[71] The Guardian). Retrieved on December 15, from: By ending the Iran deal, Trump has put America on the path to war | Bernie Sanders | The Guardian.

[72] Thomas L. Friedman. Trump Iran Policy has Become a disaster for the U.S. and Israel. New York Times, November 30, 2021. Retrieved from: Opinion | Trump's Iran Policy Has Become a Disaster for the U.S. and Israel - The New York Times (nytimes.com)

and cancellation until Iran potentially obtains a nuclear deterrent, resembling India, Pakistan, and North Korea.

The pressure approach on Iran is long-standing. Since the Iranian revolution in 1979 that ousted the pro-American Shah, U.S.-Iran policy has drawn in a variety of tools to deter and respond to Iran's actions-particularly its support for terrorism and expanding nuclear program against the United States and its regional partners. These tools have included sanctions, military support for Iran's adversaries, and sabotage of Iran's nuclear facilities to contain and degrade Iran's capabilities, the 2011 Stuxnet operation being a prominent example[73].

Therefore, the longstanding approach to Iran's nuclear program and the country, dating back to 1979, is outdated and ineffective in achieving its intended objectives. The global and regional geopolitical landscape has undergone significant changes since then, necessitating a reevaluation of the U.S. policy toward Iran. Initially, when the Ayatollah regime came to power in 1979 following the Islamic Revolution, the United States adopted a strategy focused on using the religious regime as a buffer against the Soviet Union's expansionism, especially during its invasion of Afghanistan. This strategy aimed to safeguard U.S. interests in Saudi Arabia and other Arab Gulf nations with vital oil resources. The Soviet Union no longer exists, and the U.S. has left Afghanistan. Thus, political reform in Iran helps the United States attain its

---

[73] Council on Foreign Relations, "Stuxnet," webpage, July 2010.

strategic objectives in the region and safeguard and foster its interests. In hindsight, the opportunity for such reform was missed in 2009 when President Obama did not support the Green Revolution in Iran and excluded Iran from his New Middle East political reform and democratic change initiative in MENA. Also, President Biden missed a similar opportunity in supporting the 2022 uprising following the killing of a woman activist, Mahsa Amini, who challenged the regime by advocating for Iranian women's freedom.

Acknowledging the changing dynamics in the region and reassessing the approach to Iran becomes imperative for the United States to effectively navigate and safeguard its interests in the evolving geopolitical landscape. In his book "World Order," Henry Kissinger stated that: "The United States can be a crucial factor in determining whether Iran pursues the path of revisionary Islam or that of a great nation legitimately and notably lodged in the Westphalian system of states. But America can fulfill the role only based on involvement, not withdrawal; no serious regional strategy can ignore a power as necessary as Iran"[74].

---

[74] Kissinger, H. World Order. Random House, New York. 2015. P. 169.

RIAD S. AISAMI

The U.S. and Iran Nuclear Program and Its Influence in the Region

"Summary, Conclusions, and Recommendations"

Preventing Iran from acquiring nuclear weapons presents a multifaceted challenge for the U.S., especially given the existing atomic capabilities of Israel and other regional players. Addressing Iran's nuclear ambitions requires a broader, multilateral strategy due to the interconnected nature of atomic dynamics in the region. The prospect of maintaining peaceful coexistence between Israel and Iran is diminishing as Iran advances towards acquiring nuclear capabilities. Israel, driven by concerns for its security and regional dominance, finds it untenable to accept a nuclear-armed Iran. Conversely, Iran is unwilling to relinquish its ambition to become a nuclear state for reasons mirroring Israel's self-defense and the pursuit of regional influence. Adding complexity to the situation, Iran is surrounded by four nuclear states in its neighborhood: India, Pakistan, Russia, and China. This geopolitical landscape intensifies the security considerations for both Israel and Iran, contributing to the escalating tensions in the region. Also, the task of curbing Iran's influence is closely tied to restoring the disrupted geopolitical balance resulting from the U.S. invasion of Iraq and the ongoing conflict in Syria.

The United States faces the intricate challenge of addressing immediate concerns about Iran while navigating broader regional dynamics that shape its influence. Given the Middle East's complex geopolitical landscape, a comprehensive, multi-step strategy is indispensable. While preventing Iran's nuclear ambitions and containing its influence are crucial, a narrow focus on these aspects may only prove insufficient considering the broader regional dynamics and power balances, including resolving the Arab-Israeli conflict. However, the United States must engage in a diplomatic and strategic approach to foster stability and restore the geopolitical balance in the Middle East. Such an approach recognizes the complex interplay of geopolitical factors, especially the evolving relations among Iran, Saudi Arabia, and other Arab Gulf States.

Also, the United States must pay particular attention to the evolving alliances between Iran and major global powers such as Russia and China, which wield substantial influence over U.S. Middle East strategies. Before the 1979 Islamic Revolution that ousted the Shah, Iran was a vital U.S. ally in the region. At that time, the U.S. strategically utilized the Iranian religious regime as a buffer between the Soviet Union in Afghanistan and the vital oil sources in Saudi Arabia and other Arab Gulf States. Given the significant geopolitical shifts in the region and globally, the United States must reintegrate Iran —the state —into its updated Middle East strategy. Failure to do so could prompt Iran, the regime, to consider alternative alliances with Russia and China. The current Iranian Mullahs regime is considered outdated, urging the U.S. to explore avenues for fostering gradual political reforms in Iran.

Chapter 5: The United States and the Russian Challenge

After the September 11, 2001, attacks, President George W. Bush declared a war on terror, leading to the occupation of Afghanistan and later Iraq. Throughout his eight years in office, there was increased pressure on Iran, with the possibility of an airstrike before he left office[75].

Neoconservative figures in President Bush Jr.'s administration, including Vice President Dick Cheney and Defense Secretary Donald Rumsfeld, utilized the post-9/11 environment to pursue their goal of controlling the geographical area between the former Soviet Union and Gulf oil sources. The neocon project aimed to extend US influence from the Arabian Sea to the Caspian Sea, creating a buffer zone between Russia's southern and China's western borders. The map of the region at the time showed a widespread American presence, except for Iran. Then, the United States had a multifaceted presence in Somalia, including humanitarian aid and the safeguarding of navigation in the Bab al-Mandab Strait. Additionally, the US was engaged in Yemen against

---

[75] James Joyner. Some Generals May Quit if Bush Orders Iran's Attack. Outside the Beltway. Published on Sunday February 25, 2007. Retrieved from: Some Generals May Quit if Bush Orders Iran Attack – Outside the Beltway.

al-Qaeda, maintaining logistical bases in Oman and the UAE, central military bases in Qatar, Saudi Arabia, Kuwait, and Iraq, and stationing the Fifth Fleet in Bahrain. There were military and intelligence bases in Afghanistan, Turkey, and Central Asian republics[76], as shown in Fig. 5 below.

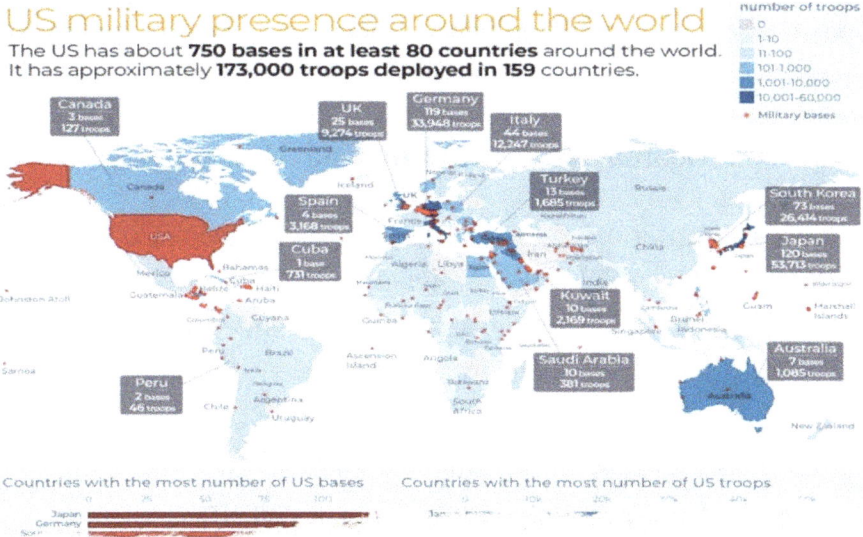

Figure 5, the U.S. Military Presence in the Middle East and worldwide after September 11, 2001.

Figure 5: The American Military Presence in the Middle East Region after September 11, 2001.

Russian President Putin observed U.S. actions near Russian borders, NATO expansion, and regime changes in the Middle East

---

[76] Retrieved from Aljazeera Website: Infographic: US military presence around the world | Infographic News | Al Jazeera.

and North Africa. Therefore, Russia strategically supported the Syrian regime, gaining leverage over the U.S. in the Syrian crisis and influencing broader issues like Crimea, Ukraine, and European power dynamics. Russia's stake in Syria was a key bargaining chip in international relations and competition with China and the United States. Losing control over the Syrian crisis would jeopardize Russia's positions and interests in multiple geopolitical arenas.

President Obama's Anti-War Doctrine

Upon assuming office in 2009, President Barack Obama aimed to shape new post-Cold War policies, with a focus on eliminating terrorism and resolving the Arab-Israeli conflict. However, his efforts included attempting to halt Israeli settlements and faced resistance from Israeli Prime Minister Netanyahu, as discussed in chapter three. As events unfolded, a significant shift occurred in the geopolitical landscape. Israel found common ground with Russia, particularly amid the Syrian crisis. This alignment between Israel and Russia, rooted in shared interests in restoring Cold War dynamics, elevated Israel's role as a strategic player in the Middle East. Unfortunately, this strategic partnership came at the expense of U.S. regional influence. This realignment of alliances became evident in the Syrian conflict, where Israel played a crucial role while Russia emerged as a critical peace broker. The Syrian regime, along with Iran and Russia, acted with a sense of impunity, perceiving a reluctance on the part of the U.S. and President Obama to employ military force. This perception was further underscored by Russia's bold move into Crimea in 2014, conducted with confidence in the absence of anticipated military repercussions from the United States. The narrative points to a complex interplay of geopolitical forces, with the evolving relationships between the U.S., Israel, and Russia shaping dynamics in the Middle East, particularly during the Syrian crisis and its aftermath[77].

President Trump and Putin Meeting in Helsinki

Due to his anti-war doctrine, President Obama faced challenges in effectively countering President Putin's actions, including the occupation of Crimea in 2014[78]. Also, the response to Russian interference in the U.S. election during Obama's tenure was criticized as inadequate by President Trump, despite benefiting from this interference, also failed to confront Putin decisively[79].

During President Trump's first meeting with President Putin, he shocked lots of people by absolving Russia of election interference, criticizing the CIA, and blaming the Obama

---

[77] Aisami, R. "Obama is Departing, and the Middle East is in Flames." Arab Scientific Publishers, Inc. Beirut, Lebanon, 2017, pp.274-275.

[78] The Long, destructive Shadow of Obama's Russian Doctrine. A series of bad decisions during the Obama years prepared the ground for Vladimir Putin's war. By Adrian Karatnycky. Foreran Policy (FP), June 18, 2012 .

[79] Bipartisan Senate report urges presidents to "put aside politics" to fight election interference. BY OLIVIA GAZIS. CBS NEWS. UPDATED ON: FEBRUARY 6, 2020/ 3:16 PM EST .

administration for poor cooperation with Russia. These actions were widely criticized as disgraceful and even treasonous, raising concerns about the U.S.'s ability to manage Russian challenges in Ukraine, Syria, and beyond. President Trump praised Putin as a "good competitor" and downplayed the investigation by Robert Mueller. "It dominated headlines for two years, but in March 2019, special counsel Robert Mueller's probe into Russian meddling in the 2016 election ended. The investigation, which President Donald Trump continually called a "witch hunt," found no evidence that Trump's campaign colluded with Russia but fell short of completely exonerating the president[80]. President Trump's praise for Putin faced criticism from Political elites, both Democrats and Republicans, including then Speaker of the House Paul Ryan and Republican Senator Jeff Flake, who found President Trump's behavior unacceptable.

The criticism centered on a press conference with Putin after their meeting in Helsinki, which was considered profoundly concerning. Former CIA Director John Brennan asserted that Trump's behavior amounted to national treason, emphasizing the need for accountability. Democratic Party leaders speculated about Putin possessing damaging information about President Trump before details of the closed-door meeting between them became public. The closed-door meeting, lasting four hours and held

---

[80] Abby Johnston and Leila Miller. The Mueller Investigation, Explained. BPC, March 25, 2019. Retrieved from: The Mueller Investigation, Explained | FRONTLINE (pbs.org)

contrary to customary protocol, needed an official recording or minutes. The disclosed information included an agreement to collaborate on preventing the spread of nuclear weapons and regarding China as a mutual friend. Putin also subtly undermined the U.S.'s approach to the Syrian conflict in the presence of President Trump. Retired General Philip M. Breedlove, the former commander of NATO forces in Europe, penned "NATO's Next Step," published in the July-August 2016 American Foreign Affairs Magazine.

In his article, Breedlove warned about the dangers of complacency in dealing with President Putin and stressed the critical importance of monitoring Putin's movements towards Europe. The General emphasized the need for vigilance and strategic awareness in the face of potential geopolitical challenges, urging an initiative-taking approach to address the evolving security landscape. He stated, "Our actions represent a strong start, but it is not enough. This is because the foundations of any strategy we have in Europe must be based on the realization that Russia represents an existential threat to the United States, Europe, and its allies. And to the global system. Russia is determined to re-emerge as a global superpower, and Putin expressed this ambition more than once. Examples of his ambitions include simulating a provocative attack on US forces, which was represented by harassing the battleship "USS Donald Cook" in the Baltic Sea last April. They also tried to restore the atmosphere of the Cold War by flying bombers along the coast of the United States. And whether it could be more of a show of force than Russia's blatant intervention in Syria. Moscow is determined to use any opportunity to expand its influence beyond its borders because the Kremlin views the United States and other NATO countries as primary adversaries. He also considers his relationship with the West to be a zero-sum equation. He also asserts that the United States must force Russia to change its calculations before it commits an even greater foolishness[81].

Biden's G7 Summit and Meeting with Putin

President Biden's interactions with President Putin were evident during his first foreign trip on June 13, 2021, which included the G7 Summit in Cornwall, the NATO Summit in Brussels, and a significant meeting with Russian President Vladimir Putin in Geneva on June 15, 2021[82]. President Biden's approach to the G7 Summit appeared rooted in a Cold War mentality, reminiscent of the alliance's founding in 1949. This was despite the significant shift in the geopolitical landscape, with Germany now a strong country and the largest economy in Europe. President Biden's attempt to leverage the G7 against China was criticized, even from traditional U.S. allies in Europe. Contrary to President Nixon's strategic brilliance in navigating Cold War dynamics, President Biden needed a sharp vision and strategic plan for dealing with

---

[81] Breedlove, P. M. NATO's Next Step. An article published in the American Foreign Affairs Magazine, the July-August issue, 2016.

[82] Biden's experience with Russia, in key moments from 1973 to now. Y Christopher Hickey. CNN, 11:40 AM EDT, Wed June 16, 2021.

Russia and China, aspiring to play significant roles in the new world order.

Currently, European countries face economic challenges due to shifting global conflict factors, and the European Union strives to safeguard its economic power by maintaining balanced relations with China. Additionally, it seeks to preserve military strength through NATO without engaging in direct conflict with Russia, a significant military force nearby. Thus, President Biden's first foreign meetings yielded little tangible outcome.

Biden vs. Putin

Anticipations were cautious, given the history of strained relations between the two leaders, dating back to when Mr. Biden was Vice President under President Obama. Despite a contentious issue between the U.S. and Russia, ranging from the occupation of Crimea and invasion of Ukraine to the Syrian crisis and Iran's nuclear ambitions, the primary focus was expected to be on Russia's interference in U.S. internal affairs. Biden, known for his commitment to standing up to Putin, labeled him a murderer in a press conference. The four-hour meeting with Putin took the form of an organized warning rather than a dialogue, unlike the Trump-Putin meeting in 2018. The post-meeting press conferences were held separately, a choice made by Biden to avoid potential disagreements in front of journalists. However, in the period leading to Russia's invasion of Ukraine on February 24, 2022, President Biden stepped up his criticism of the Russian President, warned of his intention to invade Ukraine, and threatened to impose more sanctions on Russia if Mr. Putin ordered an invasion of Ukraine. President Putin, for his part, warned President Biden that any economic sanctions imposed on Russia if it moves to take new military action against Ukraine could result in a "complete rupture" of relations between the two nuclear superpowers[83].

Putin Attempts to Control the Gas Markets

President Vladimir Putin's current strategy in the Middle East and Eastern Europe centers on enhancing Russia's global standing amid the rivalry between the United States and China for world leadership. A vital aspect of this strategy is gaining control over significant gas resources and influencing global gas prices, akin to the U.S.'s historical approach to oil dominance since World War II. Putin's objective today is to reverse this dynamic, challenging the equation that contributed significantly to U.S. success and supremacy in the 20th century. In her book "The Emperor of Gas," Russian journalist Natalia Gharib argues that Putin has transformed Russia's energy sector into a tool to pressure the European Union and destabilize neighboring former Soviet countries. Putin aims to extend this influence on more distant regions, including the Middle East, strategically controlling transportation and gas supply routes to Europe. Putin's strategy involves geopolitical maneuvering and control over strategic

---

[83] New York Times. Putin Warns Biden of 'Complete Rupture' of U.S.-Russia Relationship Over Ukraine. By David E. Sanger and Andrew E. Kramer. Dec. 30, 2021.

points to exert influence and challenge the traditional dominance of the United States in key global regions[84].

Nikita Sokolov from the Washington Institute for Near East Policy believes that Syria's gas and oil production is insignificant compared to other countries in the region, such as Iran, Qatar, and other Gulf states. However, what Putin was interested in reaching Syria was the expected future gas production on the Syrian and Lebanese coasts and preventing the Qatari gas from reaching Europe. That is why, after the military entry into Syria in 2015, the Russian company Soyuz Oil Gas won a procurement that had already been settled in its favor to explore gas in the Syrian maritime areas near the Turkish border[85].

Before becoming entangled in the conflict with Ukraine, Russia explored potential coordination with Israel to influence the future of gas production along the Lebanese coast. Iran, through its ally Hezbollah, exerts control over Lebanon's government and crucial decisions, including those related to gas production. This indicates Russia's efforts to establish control over gas sources across the Middle East, along with their transportation and marketing points. Therefore, the United States appears hesitant to leave the Syrian

---

[84] Gharib, N. Gas Emperor, a book Russian translated into Arabic, published by Madbouly Bookshop in Egypt, 2019.

[85] Sokolov, N. The energy goals of Russia in Syria. The Washington Institute for Near East Policy, August 30, 2017.

arena, especially given Russia's expanding influence in the region. The ongoing geopolitical dynamics and strategic interests are influencing the decisions and actions of major players in the Middle East. Also, the Russian invasion of Ukraine has profoundly impacted the global energy market, leading to price volatility due to supply shortages. The Middle East, the largest oil producer, has been able to capitalize on the situation[86].

Promptly, the United States requested that Saudi Arabia increase oil production to reduce prices and put more pressure on Russia. However, Saudi Arabia rejected the request, leading to a standoff between the countries. Thus, the United States increased its oil production. The U.S. crude oil export in the first half of 2023 averaged 3.9 million barrels daily, a record high since the first half

---

[86] Ewan Thomson. 6 Ways Russian's invasion of Eucain shaped the energy world. World Economic Forum. November 2022. Retrieved from: 6 ways Ukraine war led energy crisis reshaped the world | World Economic Forum (weforum.org).

of 2015[87]. However, the relationship between Saudi Arabia, China, and Russia is also crucial in the future of Oil prices[88].

Lawrence Freedman defines strategy as the art of creating power[89]. This definition dramatically applies to President Vladimir Putin's military involvement in Syria in 2015. Putin's primary motivation was to develop and exercise power, positioning Russia as a global force without risking a world war with the West. Historically, Syria has been a strategic center in the Middle East, providing Putin with an ideal geostrategic base from which to challenge the United States. Putin recognizes that regional tensions must persist in maintaining influence in the Middle East and is willing to function as a firefighter. However, Putin faces challenges, particularly with increasing Western sanctions against Russia and warnings to Western companies against investing in the country, exacerbated by the Russian invasion of Ukraine. The

---

[87] U.S. Crude Oil Export Reached Record High in the First Half of 2023. U.S. Energy Information Administration. Annual Report, December 2023. Homepage - U.S. Energy Information Administration (EIA).

[88] Vivek Y Kelkar. Money Control, December 15, 23. Retrieved from: Saudi Arabia, China, and Russia: The fateful triangle that decides the future of oil prices (moneycontrol.com).

[89] 12 Minutes. Strategy PDF Summary – Lawrence Freedman. Strategy Summary – Lawrence Freedman. Emir Zecovic | Posted on June 8, 2018. Retrieved from: Strategy PDF Summary - Lawrence Freedman | 12min Blog.

reality is complex, surpassing the capabilities of Putin's limited and short-term strategies in the Middle East. Despite economic costs to Russia, it has achieved victories in Syria at the expense of Turkey and Iran, imposing new rules of engagement that challenge the United States. Putin seeks political victories on the international stage, aiming to leverage these gains to lift Western sanctions. However, achieving this goal remains elusive and might risk escalating tensions with the West, potentially pushing Russia closer to China. Putin bets that Russia's power in Syria can prompt the United States to make concessions, leading to a balanced relationship with Europe. However, a forceful pursuit of this goal could entangle Russia in a cold war with the West and align it more closely with China in the ongoing global rivalry. In conclusion, the United States will not be able to win the battle with Russia in Crimea and Ukraine and continue to protect Europe and sustain NATO if it does not win with it in Syria and deprive President Putin of a decisive influence in the Middle East.

The U.S. and the Russian Challenge

"Summary, Conclusions, and Recommendations"

Addressing the challenges posed by Russia requires a comprehensive approach from the U.S. Effectively dealing with the ongoing Syrian conflict is pivotal, necessitating a blend of diplomatic initiatives, negotiations, and potential concessions, coupled with a willingness to deploy military force if required. A resolution in Syria that aligns with U.S. interests could diminish Russia's influence in the region. Successful diplomacy is crucial to navigating the intricacies of the Syrian conflict, engaging in meaningful negotiations with Russia, and avoiding dire and costly military confrontation. This approach involves understanding the concerns of all parties, identifying common ground, and being open to making feasible concessions. Concurrently, the U.S. should maintain preparedness to use military force strategically to protect its interests and secure a favorable outcome in Syria. By adopting a balanced strategy that combines diplomatic efforts with a credible military deterrent, the U.S. can bolster its ability to counter Russia's challenges in the Middle East and prepare for the more complex strategic competition with China, as discussed in the subsequent chapter.

Regardless of all the aid that Ukraine is receiving from Europe and the United States, it is not expected to defeat Russia in the ongoing war for almost two years. Direct participation by the United States and NATO in this war will drag it into a long, costly, and catastrophic war. The U.S. Congress is divided on Ukraine and is not expected to approve President Biden's continuous requests for aid. Thus, the U.S. administration should facilitate an end to this war as soon as possible and help reduce the signing of new security and mutual relations agreements between Russia and Europe. This move can help address the Russian challenge to the U.S. in Syria and the Middle East.

Chapter 6: The United States and Competition with China

China launched the Belt and Road Initiative (BRI) in the fall of 2013, set an operational plan for it in 2015, and included it in its Constitution in 2017 as part of China's national long-term strategic plan. Through this initiative, China sought to restore and expand on the ancient Silk Roads and build an intertwined, continuous network of land, sea, and railways to transport Chinese goods to the world. Most observers believe that China aims from this initiative, in the short term and beyond, to have economic control over the world because of its accelerated economic growth. This situation could also lead to political and military control due to the tremendous development of technology in China and the multiplicity and diversity of its uses in all areas of life. China's initiative focuses on projects that include establishing and developing the necessary infrastructure for the countries through which the Chinese Silk Roads facilitate the arrival of Chinese goods to the intended stations. Therefore, it relies on investment in building roads, bridges, tunnels, and seaports. The countries that expressed their desire to be part of the Chinese initiative have reached over seventy-two countries, fifty-six countries in the three continents (Asia, Africa, and Europe)[90].

China and the Middle East

Since the launch of the Belt and Road Initiative (BRI) in 2013, China has been seeking to expand its influence in the Middle East, where the United States has been overwhelmingly present since the end of World War II. China realizes it will only win its global conflict with the United States if it gains influence in the Middle East, the world's most critical geostrategic region, from which it can reach all continents. Therefore, China was keen to conclude long-term investment and cooperation treaties with most Middle Eastern countries, including Israel, Iran, Turkey, Saudi Arabia, the United Arab Emirates (UAE), and the other Gulf countries, as well as Iraq and Syria. The PRC (People's Republic of China) imports half of its oil from the Middle East and is the top oil customer of Saudi Arabia and Iran. The Middle East and North Africa Treaty (MENAT) represent the cornerstone of the PRC's Belt and Road Initiative (BRI), accounting for 28.5% of its investments in 2021. The PRC has strategic partnerships with five MENAT states (Algeria, Egypt, Iran, Saudi Arabia, and the UAE) and with seven (Iraq, Jordan, Kuwait, Morocco, Oman, Qatar, and Turkey). From 2005 to 2022,

---

[90] Based on China's Massive Belt and Road Initiative. Backgrounder written by James McBride and Andrew Chatzky, published by the Council on Foreign Relations on: https://www.cfr.org/backgrounder/chinas-massive-belt-and-road-initiative. Last updated on February 2, 2023.

PRC investments and contracts in the MENAT (Middle East, North Africa, and Turkey) totaled $273 billion. In 2021, Chinese investment in the region increased 360%, while construction rose 116% relative to 2020[91].

The Chinese Israeli Cooperation

The treaty China signed with Israel was the most important it entered into in the Middle East because of Israel's close relationship with the United States and its ability to serve as a balancing force in the region's geopolitical equation. In addition to China's new relationship with Russia, which has become a key player in the Syrian crisis and Middle Eastern affairs.

On October 11, 2023, China Briefing Outlook stated that: *"Over the past two decades, trade of goods and services between China and Israel has increased significantly. China presently stands as Israel's second-largest trading partner, with the total trade value reaching US$24.45 billion, marking an 11.6 percent increase in 2022 compared to the previous year.*

---

[91] China Regional Snapshot: Middle East and North Africa. U.S. Congress Foreign Affairs Committee Report published on:

https://foreignaffairs.house.gov/china-regional-snapshot-middle-east-and-north-africa/ last updated 10/25/2022.

Between 2019 and 2022, trade between the two countries underwent a significant upsurge, marking an increase of US$6.41 billion, which accounted for a 57 percent growth.

This substantial rise primarily stemmed from imports from China, which escalated from US$6.79 billion in 2019 to US$13.12 billion in 2022, signifying a substantial US$6.33 billion increase.

As of 2022, only a tiny percentage of China's overall foreign investment is directed to Israel, and the country's growth rate is also lower than China's overall growth rate for foreign investment. China has boosted its average yearly investment in Israel since 2002, with the annual investment growing from US$20 million to more than US$200 million.

Data from the Institute of National Security Studies shows that China's investments and M&As in Israel were overwhelmingly directed to the technology sector (449 deals with a reported value of US$9.14 billion up to 2019)[92].

These numbers and statistics must concern the United States as a whole. However, this economic and trade cooperation between China and Israel should not worry the United States. Instead, China invested in the two largest arms exporters in Israel. They are Israel

---

[92] China-Israel Bilateral Trade and Investment Outlook. Written by Giulia Interesse, and reported by China Briefing Outlook on October 11, 2023. Retrieved from: https://www.china-briefing.com/news/china-israel-investments-trade-outlook-belt-and-road-initiative/

Aerospace Industries and arms manufacturer Rafael. The state of Israel owns both and has subsidiaries in the United States. These two companies help manufacture the most advanced Israeli weapons, especially missiles, electronics, and aviation. However, security observers believe that China is using Israel as a backdoor to access and penetrate the most advanced covert programs of the United States. Chinese construction companies are also expanding Israel's two main ports of Haifa and Ashdod. These contracts aroused U.S. concern because the Chinese companies have obtained concessions to operate and manage the two new ports for 25 years. They are the most critical Israeli naval bases in Israel. The heavily fortified Israeli naval infrastructure is in them, including the submarine fleet. The U.S. Navy conducts joint operations with the Israeli Navy in the port of Haifa from time to time[93].

The Israeli and Palestinian beaches, starting with Gaza Shore in the south and ending with Haifa Beach in the north, could represent the future essential trading centers for China on the Mediterranean, as they are accessible to Europe, are close to the Red Sea, and cross into Africa. Therefore, Israel was among the first countries in the Middle East to be included in the Chinese initiative and to sign partnership contracts with the Chinese-backed Asian Infrastructure Bank. According to Israeli researchers specializing in future studies, Israel will be the biggest winner from the Chinese

---

[93] The Belt and Road Initiative and the inevitability of Arab geography. A study by Muhammad Makram Balawi. Al Jazeera Night, October 7, 2107.

initiative. It can provide modern ports, advanced rail networks, and efficient administrative systems. It does not require too much time or effort to integrate with the proposed Chinese projects in the region, unlike most other Arab and Asian countries included in the Belt and Road Initiative. So that Israel can provide a ready-to-use landline from the port of Eilat, overlooking the Red Sea, to other ports such as Ashdod, Ashkelon, and Haifa along the coast that Israel controls on the Mediterranean Sea. Therefore, the continuation of normalizing the relations between the Arab countries and Israel, started by President Trump, will be in China's interest. Such a situation makes China eligible to play an essential role in the future peace process between the Israelis and the Palestinians, which will flow into its intended economic role in the region. Such a situation can make China a more credible mediator in the Arab-Israeli conflict than the United States[94].

Trade Cooperation Agreements Between China and Iran

The trade agreement signed by China with Iran on March 24, 2021, strengthened the distinguished relations between the two countries. This indicates a new geopolitical alignment aimed at confronting American influence in the Middle East. It is also a new way to relieve the suffocating pressure on the Iranian economy, which is facing unprecedented challenges due to international sanctions led by the United States, which reached their highest levels after former President Donald Trump unilaterally canceled

---

[94] Based on a study published on Al-Arabiya.net on November 10, 2021.

the nuclear agreement with Iran. President Joe Biden has yet to secure Iran's return to the deal President Barack Obama signed in 2015, when he was vice president and played a distinguished role in reaching it. However, China and Iran's trade and economic relations have existed for a while. It extends back to the nineties of the last century, after the fall of the Soviet Union. China has become a significant trading partner for Iran over the past two decades. Thus, the total trade between them has increased in recent years to about $20 billion annually. Iran's exports to China amounted to about $8.9 billion. And Iran's imports from China amounted to approximately 9.7 billion. Thus, China has become Iran's leading industrial supplier and one of its largest oil importers. In 2016, following Chinese President Xi Jinping's official visit to Iran, Xi met with the Iranian Supreme Leader, Ali Khamenei, and the two countries agreed to intensify cooperation and increase bilateral trade to $400 billion within 10 years. In June 2020, a draft proposal for a "comprehensive strategic partnership" between China and Iran leaked to the media. The sources indicated the determination of both countries to pursue a broader partnership that includes cooperation in the economic, political, cultural, and military fields over the next twenty-five years. China pledges to invest $400 billion in Iran's oil, gas, and transport infrastructure[95].

---

[95] China-Iran Relations: A limited but Enduring Partnership. U.S.-China Economic and Security Review Commission. Staff Research Report, June 28, 2021. Retrieved from: China-Iran Relations: A Limited but Enduring Strategic Partnership (uscc.gov)

Speaking to Al-Jazeera International Podcasting Network in March 2021, Barbara Slaven, an expert on Iranian affairs and director of the Future of Iran Initiative at the Atlantic Council, said: "China is trying to expand its presence and influence in the Middle East. China has already become the region's first trading partner. The outbreak of the COVID-19 virus provided China with an opportunity to exploit vaccine diplomacy to leverage its regional influence." However, Slaven believes that China's regional goal is more limited than that of the United States, which has allies and partners. At the same time, it is committed to providing a regional security umbrella for the countries with which it deals. This proposition is also supported by Professor John Calabrese, an expert on China-Middle East relations at American University in Washington, who notes that Washington enjoys broad military and diplomatic influence in the Middle East. Still, the challenge will be how China can play the role of helping regional adversaries by finding common ground with them and continuing to achieve balance in its relationships with them[96].

This comes when the Chinese-American conflict exacerbates other issues in the Middle East and the world, including digital technology, communications, and intellectual property rights. Along with them are disputes over navigation in the South China Sea, political repression in Hong Kong, human rights abuses of the

---

[96] The Chinese Iranian agreement... Why is it such a massive surprise for Washington? A study by Muhammad Al-Minshawi, Al-Jazeera Net, 3-30-2021.

Muslims in Xinjiang, and the fate of Taiwan. In addition to the coronavirus pandemic and its aftermath, China has consistently sought to reassure the United States that strengthening relations with Iran will not increase its influence in the Middle East. Although this agreement strengthens Chinese-Iranian ties, other countries in the region, such as those in the Arab Gulf states, will continue to be an essential part of China's basic orientation toward importing the energy needed for its industry. And to secure the logistical routes for Chinese trade to the world, given these countries' geographical locations. China must maintain this geostrategic balance to achieve strategic competition with the United States in the region. This is evident in the extent of China's distinguished partnership with the United Arab Emirates. Whether in developing and using commercial ports, such as Jebel Ali Port. This agreement means that China is an essential and dependable partner to the UAE. Researchers also noted that the comprehensive strategic partnership between China and the United Arab Emirates in 2018 has evolved into a strategic alliance capable of achieving tangible results in the future. Therefore, China always seeks new regional partners and uses the "comprehensive strategic partnership" concept in all its bilateral agreements. Also, the Chinese agreements are a strategic cooperation that meets common interests. This also applies to the Chinese Iranian cooperation agreements. However, China continues to be cautious in its relationship with Iran. This is to avoid binding commitments to Iran, which would put it in an embarrassing position given the tense relationship between Iran and the West. And not to provoke the United States prematurely in its historical influence in the Middle East. Thus, China tries to get as close to any country in the

Middle East as the United States tries to get away from it. For example, when the United States began to reduce its military presence in Saudi Arabia and delayed selling advanced arms, as happened with the F-35 Aircraft and ballistic missile deal, China agreed to Saudi Arabia's request to build an advanced ballistic missile system.

The Middle East and its Geostrategic Importance to the Implementation of China's Belt and Road Initiative

China's Belt and Road Initiative (BRI) includes six lines. The majority pass through the Middle East, which makes China pay close attention to the region. Therefore, Chinese foreign policy in the Middle East focuses on stable, calm countries, regardless of the nature and governance style of their regimes. China does not espouse ideologies and does not try to force them on others, as the Soviet Union did during the Cold War. China has flexibility with the outside and shows political pragmatism that supports and promotes its economic interests, which have become the basis of its superiority and provide effective means in its global conflict with the United States. Therefore, what China cares about in its foreign trade policy is the geography of its trading regions and the stability of its markets. As well as the freedom of movement of goods, their transfer from one place to another, and their easy access to the targeted consumers. Based on observing China's foreign policy approach and the trade deals she seeks throughout the world, we may be able to conclude that China is using the "Belt and Road" initiative as leverage to control the world economically and push the United States away from the areas that she seeks to dominate, hoping, along with Russia, to squeeze the U.S. within its continental borders and take her back to where it was before it turned into a global power after entering World War I in 1917. So, this would divide the world into two landmasses on either side of the Atlantic Ocean. In this case, China can lead the new world order, as it controls the world's most significant, populous, and essential part. And if China succeeds in doing so, it will end the current World Order led by the United States alone, with European support and global influence, since the end of World War II. However, China's dilemma stems from its unfavorable neighbors, prominent and influential countries shaping the international system, such as India, Japan, South Korea, Australia, Vietnam, the Philippines, and Taiwan. Also, the main land route in the Belt and Road Initiative that crosses into Europe must go through Russia, a traditional enemy of Chinese hegemony worldwide. And, under Putin's leadership, it aspired to have a balanced role in the new world order. This is due to its large area and geographical location between the continents of Asia and Europe. It can be a balancing figure in the Chinese American conflict equation today. However, Russia cannot stop China from moving at full speed toward the new world order, and it can only hinder its acceleration and seek to be its main driving force. This comes at a time when milestones in military and energy cooperation are necessary for the economic growth of the southeastern countries near the Strait of Malacca, which lies at the entrance to the South China Sea. The Strait of Malacca is where 80% of China's oil and food needs pass through, and where the same proportion of its exports to the world come out: The United States and a group of its allies, including Australia and the United Kingdom, who oppose the Chinese hegemony, control this vital waterway—established the "AUKUS" naval alliance. It may also expand later to other countries that are friends with the U.S. and share the same interests, such as New Zealand and Japan. It may also reach out to other maritime countries friendly to the United States near the Indian and Pacific oceans. And so, this alliance poses a severe threat to China. Therefore, China seeks to reduce its effectiveness as much as possible and quietly. By expanding and activating the road circuit. Whether through the movement of goods out of its periphery or the import of energy from Russia and Central Asia through pipelines. The Chinese Silk Road, which passes through the republics of Central Asia, also passes through Turkey via either highways or railways. With the development of this long continental route, the train journey from China to Spain (its farthest point) now takes only 21 days, half the time of the original route. Thus, Turkey holds essential cards against China in this field. And Turkey could, under certain circumstances, work with the United States to block the Chinese push. Likewise, Turkey can play the role of China within its surroundings through its new axis with the Central Asian republics, which have a population of two hundred million and a national product estimated at $2 trillion. Turkey also has an essential leverage by putting pressure on China through the Uyghur Muslims in East Turkistan in China, who number about twenty million people within an autonomous province bordering Afghanistan[97].

Therefore, the Islamic factor in the region is what the United States must consider if it wants to win its fight with China for world leadership, as happened in its conflict with the Soviet Union before, where the United States recruited the Islamic Mujahideen in Afghanistan and supported them to fight the "atheist" Soviet Union. This is what led to the defeat of the Soviets, their humiliating exit from Afghanistan, and their subsequent loss of the Cold War to the United States. The mass of Muslims that separates China from the Mediterranean Sea is equivalent to half the world's Muslims, estimated at 1.9 billion people, whose number is expected to reach more than 2.5 billion in the second half of this century. By doing so, they will become the world's most significant religious force. However, Muslims are not a single, organized bloc. They are divided into sects, specifically Shiites and Sunnis. While Iran can represent a reference for the Shiite community, it is difficult for the Sunnis to have a solo reference represented in one country, such as Saudi Arabia or Turkey. Therefore, if Turkey or Saudi Arabia wants to build a viable strategic alliance in its immediate surroundings, it must first be based on shared economic interests, not on purely religious factors.

---

[97] The importance of Turkey in obstructing the Chinese land Silk Road through Central Asia to Syria. Basil Al-Maarawi. Ninar Press, November 2022.

The United States' Dispute with China

When Donald Trump ran for the presidency in 2016, a key focus of his campaign was correcting the relationship between China and the United States. He believed that recalibrating this relationship would bring economic support, fostering the growth and prosperity he promised Americans. For about three decades since the fall of the Soviet Union in 1991, China has positioned itself as the United States preferred economic partner. This trend began during President Bill Clinton's first term in 1993. Initially, the relationship operated based on "Politics is ours, economics is yours." However, the intricate connection between politics and economics has made this separation challenging. Two critical issues loom more significant than trade and economics in the U.S.- China relationship. Firstly, the matter of U.S. intellectual property rights has become paramount. Presently, China uses over 90 American inventions in health and technology without adequately compensating the United States. This stems from the Chinese government's failure to recognize the validity of intellectual property rights. Secondly, security concerns tied to technology, including digital programming and artificial intelligence, are at the forefront. Notably, China's use of 5G technology in devices like the Huawei smartphone raises worries about potential global surveillance[98].

---

[98] Huawei's 5G chip breakthrough needs a reality check. A self-made chip puts Huawei back in the smartphone game, but US sanctions are still hurting the company. By Zeyi Yang archive. The Technology Review,

Another concern lies in China's manipulation of its currency, which can cause inflation and economic instability, as all world currencies are linked to the dollar except for the Chinese Yuan[99]. This multifaceted dispute between the United States and China is strategic, extending beyond politics or economics. It has reached a critical juncture where a war of compatibility seems inevitable. If it occurs, this prospective conflict is expected to be selective, primarily involving advanced non-conventional weapons, excluding nuclear options.

The aim would not be absolute victory or defeat but to force both sides to the negotiating table. Recognizing China's military capabilities, which exceed those of the United States in certain areas, particularly the Air Force and Navy, it is acknowledged that China does not seek a complete military overthrow. However, China remains the United States' primary global competitor, especially in Asia. Therefore, finding common ground and settling differences with China in East Asia is crucial for the United States. This is particularly relevant as the U.S. can only maintain its

---

November 15, 2023. Retrieved from: Huawei's 5G chip breakthrough needs a reality check | MIT Technology Review.

[99] Is China Manipulating Its Currency? By Brad W. Setser, CFR Expert. Council on Foreign Relations, August 8, 2019, 3:17 pm (EST). Retrieved from: Is China Manipulating Its Currency? | Council on Foreign Relations (cfr.org).

presence in the South China Sea and East Asia by simultaneously engaging in the Middle East (West Asia).

Is the Confrontation between the United States and China a Competition or a Strategy?

Since President Nixon visited China in 1972, the U.S. has adopted an open and cooperative policy towards China. After the Cold War and the Soviet Union's fall in 1991, the relationship transitioned into a "strategic partnership" by the end of President George H.W. Bush's term, reaching its zenith during President Bill Clinton's tenure in the 1990s. The strategic partnership persisted, albeit with reduced intensity, during the early 2000s under President George W. Bush. However, significant changes occurred under President Obama, particularly after Chinese President Xi Jinping launched the Belt and Road Initiative in 2013. This marked a shift towards what has been described as "cautious strategic competition." Tensions heightened at the beginning of President Donald Trump's term in 2017, characterized by economic disputes and media confrontations.

Since taking office in early 2021, President Joseph Biden has sought to shift away from the aggressive stance set by his predecessor, President Trump, opting for a more cautious return to the policies of the Obama era. However, a comprehensive and effective strategy for the future relationship with China has yet to materialize under Biden's administration. China's ascension as a significant competitor and perceived threat to the United States has prompted widespread discussion within research centers and strategic studies, as well as among global strategists and American decision-makers. "It is hegemony and confrontation, not cooperation or competition, which dominates the core of relations between America and China, despite hopes for establishing cooperation between the two superpowers to address common challenges." Such a conclusion was the main idea of a strategic analysis prepared by Matthew Kroenig, an expert and professor at Georgetown University, deputy director of the Scowcroft Center for Strategy and Security at the Atlantic Council, and Dan Negrea, a senior fellow at the center, and published by the American Journal of the National Interest. According to this analysis, the discussion centered on "competition" between the U.S. and China. But U.S. Secretary of State Anthony Blinken had said earlier in the publication of this strategic analysis that: "The U.S. policy towards China is a mixture of cooperation, competition, and confrontation." But Kroening and Negrea addressed Mr. Blinken's assertion in their analysis by stating: "Unfortunately, Secretary Blinken was right about only a third of what he said. They emphasized that "despite high hopes for cooperation between the two countries on common challenges, the painful reality is that confrontational elements increasingly dominate China-US relations." When the U.S. National Strategy Document was released in 2017, the term "competition" between significant powers became the dominant slogan in Washington. The document acknowledges that: "The previous U.S. Strategy, which focused on trying to make China an actor and responsible player within a world order based on common denominators, has failed." Therefore, there is an urgent need for a new, more assertive, and serious approach. The Biden administration has adopted the term " strategic competition" to describe the U.S. relationship with China and pledged to prioritize the most critical and strategic areas in this relationship.

The word 'competition' is inappropriate, as any competition involves the parties concerned complying with the same agreed-upon rules. But the relationship between the United States and China, according to Korangi and Nigeria, "cannot be described as a competition because the Chinese Communist Party systematically violates generally accepted international laws and norms. In the economic field, Beijing is aggressively attacking the global economic system in defiance of its obligations under the World Trade Organization. The Chinese Communist Party also violates international humanitarian law through "crimes against humanity" and "acts of genocide" against Uyghur Muslims and other minorities in the country. Militarily, Beijing asserts control over disputed territories with its neighbors, including islands in the South China Sea. Southern, despite rulings by the Hague Court against Beijing's false claims[100].

---

[100] Why "Confrontation" with China Cannot Avoid. A study by Matthew Kroenig and Dan Negrea. published by the American Journal of the National Interest on November 26, 2021.

The U.S. and Competition with China

"Summary, Conclusions, and Recommendations"

After the collapse of the Soviet Union in 1990-1991, China strengthened itself on the same grounds that the Soviet Union fell on the economy[101]. Since then, the U.S. has found a strategic partner in China. However, after President Xi Jinping declared the Belt and Road Initiative in 2013, China became a strategic competitor to the U.S. The U.S. Also, despite the U.S.'s One-China Policy, Taiwan has become a sensitive issue between the two countries. While the U.S. does not object to a peaceful negotiation between Taiwan and China in the next few years, China insists on a speedy reunification. In the last meeting between President Biden and Chinese President Xi Jinping in the U.S., held on November 15, 2023, in Woodside, California, President Xi told President Biden that China would reunify with Taiwan. However, it was unclear whether Beijing planned to use force in its effort to reunify with Taiwan, but Xi indicated they would try to do so peacefully at first[102]. However,

---

[101] What China Learned from the Collapse of the USSR. Three key lessons have helped the Chinese Communist Party avoid following its Soviet namesake into the dustbin of history. By Kunal Sharma. The Diplomat, December 06, 2021. Retrieved from: What China Learned from the Collapse of the USSR – The Diplomat.

[102] Xi told Biden at summit that China plans to reunify with Taiwan. ABC News. U.S. President Joe Biden greets Chinese President Xi Jinping before a meeting during the Asia-Pacific Economic Cooperation (APEC) Leaders'

sustaining a U.S. presence in East Asia hinges on a nuanced and strategic approach that carefully balances commitments in East and West Asia (the Middle East). A thoughtful strategy is essential to prevent China from gaining undue influence in the Middle East while maintaining strategic competition in other regions. Also, maintaining a robust U.S. presence in East Asia requires diplomatic finesse, economic engagement, and security partnerships. The U.S. should be wary of a complete withdrawal from the Middle East, as it could create a power vacuum that other actors, including China, might exploit. Simultaneously, managing strategic competition with China in various parts of the world demands a comprehensive approach. This approach includes economic, technological, and diplomatic measures to counterbalance China's influence and uphold U.S. interests in the Middle East and globally.

Since the United States already has the one-China policy, the practicality of facilitating a peaceful resolution to the Taiwan issue will help the United States limit China's growing influence in the Middle East and lay the groundwork for resolving other disputed matters.

---

week. Nov. 15, 2023, in Woodside, Calif. Retrieved from: Xi told Biden at summit that China plans to reunify with Taiwan (msn.com)

Chapter 7: The United States and the Conflict in Syria

As discussed in Chapter Two, the Obama administration faced difficulties in supporting the Syrian people's uprising against the regime in 2013. Consequently, Syria became embroiled in a brutal conflict between the Syrian regime led by President Bashar al-Assad and the opposition forces. This conflict paved the way for the rise of the Islamic State in Syria and Iraq (ISIS). On September 10, 2014, the U.S. announced the formation of a broader international coalition to defeat the Islamic State in Syria and Iraq (ISIS)[103], and Syria became a regional and international battleground in a prolonged global war.

This chapter provides a comprehensive analysis of the actions and strategies of key international and regional players in the Middle East, focusing on the reshaping of geostrategic influence in Syria and the broader struggle for gas resources in the Mediterranean basin. The geopolitical dynamics, influenced by the actions of the United States, Russia, China, and other regional powers, contribute to the complex and volatile situation in Syria and the region.

---

[103] The U.S. Department of State. Retrieved from: About Us – The Global Coalition to Defeat ISIS - United States Department of State.

The ongoing conflict in the northern and northwest parts of Syria, as well as along the eastern border with Iraq, is increasingly recognized as a global proxy war involving major powers, particularly the United States and Russia, and active regional players, including Turkey and Iran. Israel, Saudi Arabia, the UAE, and Qatar are also participating in one way or another in this complex geopolitical struggle. The Syrian regime, led by President Bashar al-Assad, and the opposing armed factions seem to have limited or no influence over the military dynamics. Notably, the conflict is not merely a confrontation between the United States, the longstanding global power, and Russia, which seeks to reassert its influence in the region and globally. Instead, it can be viewed as an indirect battleground involving China, now a formidable challenger to U.S. dominance in the area and the world. Having rapidly emerged as a potent global player, China seeks to replace the Soviet Union and become the United States' rival, primarily on economic grounds. Since the fall of the Soviet Union in 1991, China has strategically fortified its economy, expanded global trade relationships, and opened markets across four continents[104].

Beyond the economic prowess discussed in the previous chapter, China has invested heavily in advanced security communications, digital technology, and even advanced military capabilities, including nuclear submarines, aircraft, and

---

[104] The Diplomat. What China Learned from the collapse of the USSR. By Kunal Charma. Published on December 2, 2021. Retrieved from: What China Learned from the Collapse of the USSR – The Diplomat.

hypersonic and long-range missiles. The genesis of heightened attention in China came with the launch of the Belt and Road Initiative by Chinese President Xi Jinping in 2013[105]. A report from the National Security Council during President Obama's tenure emphasized the need to shift focus from Russia to China as a significant long-term competitor to the United States[106]. While acknowledging Russia as a strong regional power, the report advocated for a policy of temporary containment against Putin[107].

In response, President Obama directed his national security team to formulate a comprehensive strategic plan to address the challenges posed by China. However, the developed plan primarily involved implicating Russian President Putin in Syria in 2015, following Russia's occupation of the Crimean Peninsula in 2014. Additionally, it included implementing a stringent economic

---

[105] Council on Foreign Relations. China's Massive Belt and Road Initiative. By James McBride, Noah Berman, and Andrew Chatzky. Retrieved from: China's Massive Belt and Road Initiative | Council on Foreign Relations (cfr.org) last updated February 2, 2023.

[106] The White House, 2017; U.S. Department of Defense, 2018.

[107] Center for Strategic International Studies. The Biden Transition and the U.S. Coopetition with China and Russia: The Crisis-Driven Need to Change the U.S. Strategy. Reported by Anthony H. Cordesman and Grace Hawing. Published on January 6, 2021. Retrieved from: The Biden Transition and U.S. Competition with China and Russia: The Crisis-Driven Need to Change U.S. Strategy (csis.org).

blockade against Russia. This strategic response reveals the complex and interconnected dynamics in the evolving global power structure, with Syria serving as a pivotal arena for geopolitical maneuvering and competition among major players[108].

In contrast, President Obama faced limitations in imposing economic sanctions on China due to the substantial trade volume between the two nations and China's role as a significant holder of U.S. government securities debt. As an alternative, President Obama, in his capacity as commander-in-chief, directed a partial relocation of U.S. Fifth Fleet troops and ships, based in Bahrain, to the South China Sea, positioning them near the Strait of Malacca — a narrow waterway between the Malaysian island of Malawi and the Indonesian island of Sumatra. This strategic waterway is a crucial commercial route connecting the South China Sea to the Indian Ocean, a critical pathway for China's 80% global shipping (import and export)[109]. Fig. 6 shows a map of the Strait of Malacca.

---

[108] Brookings. Assessing U.S.-China Relations Under the Obama Administrations. By Cheng Li. Published on August 30, 2016. Retrieved from: Assessing U.S.-China relations under the Obama administration | Brookings.

[109] China and the Malacca Dilemma. By Pawel Paszak. Warsaw Institute. Published on February 28, 2021. Retrieved from: China and the "Malacca Dilemma" | Warsaw Institute.

Refer to Fig. 6, a map of the Malacca Strait.)

Figure 6: Map of the Malacca Strait

President Obama's primary objective was to enable the U.S. to monitor China's military activities in the region and closely observe its trade movements. While the move was not intended to escalate to war, China expressed dissatisfaction with what its officials termed provocative conduct by the Obama Administration. China reiterated its claim to sovereignty over the South China Sea and emphasized its right to navigate freely. Concurrently, China repositioned its primary distribution center for goods from the Southeast to the Southwest. Additionally, China initiated the construction of a significant highway through Pakistan, connecting to the port of Gwadar in the Southeast and bypassing the Strait of Malacca. Fig. 7 below shows the Chinese routes avoiding the Malacca Strait on the region's map.

Fig. 7, A map illustrating this highway through Pakistan's geography.

Figure 7: The China Trade Highway through Pakistan

This shift allowed China to diversify its shipping routes and reduce reliance on the besieged Strait of Malacca. During this period, China capitalized on Pakistan's dissatisfaction with U.S. interference in its national security affairs, including the unilateral assassination of Osama bin Laden on Pakistani soil without prior notification. This geopolitical context influenced China's strategic decisions and further contributed to the evolving dynamics in the region.

China has strategically managed its relations with neighboring countries, such as Russia, Mongolia, Iran, Afghanistan, and Kazakhstan, to revitalize various Silk Roads. This includes the use of the M4 Highway in North-West Syria, which runs parallel to its northern border with Turkey. The M4 international highway plays a crucial role in connecting different regions of Syria under the influence of various global and regional actors. It connects the Euphrates Region in the East and Northeast, currently under the control of the United States and Kurdish forces, with the Manbij and Afrin regions in North Syria, influenced by Turkey and Syrian Opposition Allies[110].

Furthermore, the M4 links central cities and regions of Syria under the control of the Russian, Syrian Regime, and Iranian control. Notably, the M4 highway connects Aleppo in the North, close to the Turkish border, and Latakia in the West, on the Mediterranean, which houses a Russian military base. The M4 intersects with another vital international highway in Syria, the M5, near Saraqib in the Idlib Province, a contested region between Russia and Turkey. The significance of the M4 lies in its connection of major trade cities like Aleppo in Northern Syria and Mosul in Northern Iraq to the Mediterranean Coast. The global and regional parties involved in Syria, including the U.S., Russia, Turkey, and Iran, vie for control over this critical geostrategic area. China

---

[110] U.S.–Russian Competition and the M4 Highway in Syria. By Joe Macaron. Arab Center Washington DC, June 23, 2020. Retrieved from: US-Russian Competition and the M4 Highway in Syria (arabcenterdc.org).

closely monitors this area as a major trading nation and is gradually entering it. Following President Biden's announcement of the U.S. troop withdrawal from Afghanistan, China contacted the Taliban to construct a road starting from its goods distribution center in Northwest China.

This road passes through Pakistan and Afghanistan, facilitated by the agreement with Iran. The route extends to Mosul in Iraq, where the M4 currently ends. The M4 road is poised to become one of the key Chinese Silk Roads, connecting China to the Mediterranean via the vital Port of Latakia in Syria. This strategic move allows China to ship goods to North Africa and Central and Western Europe. China aims for homogeneity in the Middle East and a gradual replacement of U.S. influence. Russia shares China's interest in reducing the U.S. presence in the Middle East. However, Russia faces a dilemma in Syria, where it must contend with Iran for control over "Useful Syria" and strategically deal with Turkey's influence in Idlib in Northwest Syria, where the joint path of the M4 and M5 highways is crucial to these objectives. However, Russia's involvement in the Ukrainian War made this goal more complex and costlier.

The Strategic Battle of Idlib

The Battle of Idlib, positioned as the potential decisive conflict in the Syrian proxy war, has been a subject of speculation and anticipation since the victory of Russia, Iran, and the Syrian regime in Aleppo in late 2016[111]. To control the overall situation, end the war in Syria in their favor, and impose their will, the trio has eyed Idlib as its next strategic destination. The involved parties — primarily Russia, Syria, Iran, Turkey, and the United States —have distinct goals and interests regarding the potential outcome of the battle. Russia, seeking to solidify its military strength and enhance its influence, views victory in Idlib as a means to impose a political solution that expands its areas of control. Russian President Vladimir Putin aims to use the triumph to indirectly assert influence over other parties, particularly the United States, Europe, and Turkey. Syrian President Bashar al-Assad sees an opportunity to leverage Russia's military success without making concessions to the West through the political process. Al-Assad is wary that any significant political settlement may weaken or threaten his regime. For Iran, a victory in Idlib could be a platform to alter the political landscape, reducing American and Israeli pressure and offering a more favorable international climate to address its economic crisis.

In contrast, Turkey, despite its coordination with Russia due to immediate interests, would perceive a sweeping military victory in Idlib by Russia, Iran, and the Syrian regime as a defeat. Turkey considers Idlib its backyard and has made significant investments in the region. On the other hand, the United States is cautious about

---

[111] United States Institute for Peace. Idlib: The Last Major Battle in the Syrian Civil War. By Mona Yacoubian. Published on September 5, 2018. Retrieved from: Idlib: The Last Major Battle in the Syrian Civil War | United States Institute of Peace (usip.org)

endorsing a decisive victory for Russia and Iran in Idlib, given its ongoing tensions with Iran over its nuclear program and lingering dissatisfaction with Russia's actions in Crimea and Ukraine. The Battle of Idlib, if realized, would have significant implications for the regional balance of power, as each party navigates its strategic goals and interests amid the complexities of the Syrian conflict. The map below (Fig. 8) illustrates the significance of the M4 & M5 major trade highways in Syria.

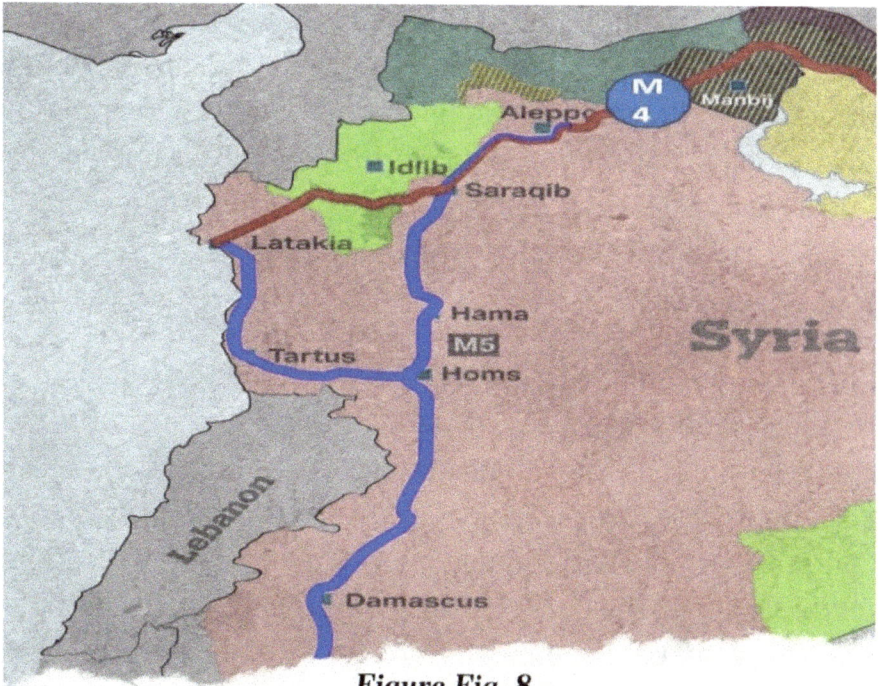

Figure Fig. 8.

Figure 8: M4 & M5 International Trade H

RIAD S. AISAMI

The U. S. and the Outcome of the Conflict in and on Syria and the Middle East

Discussions emerged within certain circles of American decision-making regarding the potential withdrawal of the United States from the Middle East or a reduction in its military presence. The proposal is to redirect attention and resources to East Asia, channeling American energies into the strategic competition with China. Consequently, there's a growing consideration of the feasibility of maintaining U.S. military bases in the region, with their focus increasingly limited to counterterrorism efforts against threats like ISIS, which no longer poses a direct threat to the U.S. Additionally, the role of securing the flow of oil, once a critical factor, is now less relevant due to changes in energy sources and the U.S.'s reduced dependence on Middle East oil.

The United States does not necessarily require a withdrawal plan from the Middle East but rather a redefined strategy to adapt to the region's changing dynamics. This conclusion was also reached by notable American strategists specializing in the Middle East. Dalia Dasa Kaye, a Senior Scientist and former Director of the Center for Middle East Public Policy at the RAND Corporation and fellow faculty at the Burke Center for International Relations at the University of California - Los Angeles, stated: "President Joe Biden's administration did not hide their intention to get out of the

Middle East"”[112]. Also, this is what Secretary of State Mr. Anthony Blinken expressed after he took over the Foreign Ministry Portfolio[113]. Dr. Kaye explained in her article that a senior official in the new Biden administration told her that, "Barack Obama's administration did not proceed with the strategy of heading towards Asia, and this is what we will do this time."

The issue of U.S. strategic competition with China has become the central focus of American foreign policy, finding bipartisan agreement in Washington, D.C., despite the city's increasing political divisions. While ongoing discourse centers on a potential U.S. withdrawal from the Middle East, the current reality points to a different scenario. The United States maintains an extensive network of military bases in the region, particularly in the Gulf states and Turkey. Moreover, the U.S. is willing to engage with all relevant regional parties to enhance regional security. The unique security umbrella provided by the United States in the Middle East is unmatched by any other country, including China or Russia.

---

[112] Foreign Affairs. America Is Not Withdrawing from the Middle East. By Dalila Dassa Kaye. Published on December 1, 2021. Retrieved from: America Is Not Withdrawing from the Middle East | Foreign Affairs.

[113] CNN Politics. The US is mounting a frantic effort to head off a wider Middle East War. Analysis by Stephen Collinson. Retrieved from: Analysis: US is mounting a frantic effort to head off a wider Middle East war | CNN Politics Updated 3:32 AM EDT, Tue October 17, 2023.

Israel's capacity to protect the Gulf states from Iran is contingent on the leadership and support of the United States[114].

Amidst increasing tensions and instability in the region, exacerbated by the inability of influential regional actors to fill the geopolitical void left by the U.S. invasion of Iraq in 2003, the Middle East remains a volatile landscape. The region stretching from Iran's borders to the Mediterranean Sea, including Iraq, Syria, and Lebanon, has become a focal point for various forms of violence, sectarian conflicts, and ethnic tensions, resembling a "black hole." Addressing this situation may necessitate the continued presence of the United States in the region. However, the U.S. must integrate its Middle East strategy into the broader competition with China for global leadership. It should aim to avoid military confrontations with Russia in Europe and emulate the post-World War II approach towards Europe through a new initiative akin to the Marshall Plan for reconstruction.

To sustain stability in the Middle East and improve living conditions for its citizens, the United States should help establish just political systems in the region. Any future president, including President Biden or his successors, must consider adopting a comprehensive Middle East strategy, learning from the efforts

---

[114] The Diplomat. Middle Eastern Countries Rebalancing Relations with the US and China. By Dale Aluf. Published on May 5, 2023. Retrieved from: Middle Eastern Countries Are Rebalancing Relations with the US and China – The Diplomat.

initiated by President Obama. Therefore, it is now the opportune moment for the United States to lead by example rather than through coercion. This approach aligns with its new strategy, which must rely on diplomacy and soft power, steering away from the brutal power tactics employed in the Middle East since the Second World War. The scope of the new American approach should not be confined to Saudi Arabia and the oil-rich Gulf states (the Gulf Cooperative Council 6 states); it should extend to Egypt and North Africa, with a specific focus on Turkey due to its unique relationship with the U.S. and its geostrategic location. Turkey is the gateway from the Middle East to central and northern Europe. It is like Egypt serves as the passage from the Middle East to North Africa and Western Europe. By holding the keys to these two gates, the United States can control crucial transit points between East and West and gain influence over entrances to the Indian and Pacific oceans, aligning with its strategy in competition with China. Additionally, such control could limit Russia's role in Eastern Europe, North Asia, and Central Asia. However, China has led the United States in forging a strategic partnership with the Middle East. This partnership is evident in the various agreements China has recently established with key Middle Eastern countries, including Israel, Iran, Turkey, Saudi Arabia, and the United Arab Emirates. The New York Times reported that the deal brokered by

China between Iran and Saudi Arabia has upended Middle East diplomacy and posed a challenge to the U.S.[115].

When President Obama left office in early 2017, the U.S. needed a clearer vision and decisive long-term strategy in Syria. The American policy focused solely on containing the situation and managing crises, leaving a void that propelled President Putin and Russia to the forefront. Russia's military presence in Syria was driven by its interest in controlling gas production in the Mediterranean, manipulating exports, and influencing prices. This strategic alignment with Russia became significant for Israel, which had emerged as a Mediterranean gas producer. Israel relied on Russia's military presence along the Syrian coast to pressure Lebanon into settling territorial disputes, complicated further by Iran's influence on Hezbollah and France's involvement after the Beirut Port explosion. Turkey also entered the scene, engaging in conflicts with both Russia and Israel over maritime borders in the Mediterranean, particularly with Cyprus, Greece, and Libya. This situation raised concerns for Russia and Israel, especially given Russia's military presence in strategic naval areas like the Aegean and Mediterranean Seas. The conflict between Russia and Turkey extended beyond Syria, encompassing broader regional competition. While they clashed over their roles in Syria and Libya,

---

[115] The New Your Times. China's Role in Iran-Saudi Arabia Deal Shows Xi's Global Goals. By David Pierson. Published on March 11, 2023. Retrieved from: China's Role in Iran-Saudi Deal Shows Xi's Challenge to U.S.-led Order-The New York Times (nytimes.co).

the potential for resolution rested on the agreement between the United States and Russia, two countries capable of addressing lingering issues without resorting to all-out war. However, a broader global conflict in the region is expected to be over the gas in the Mediterranean Basin, and the ongoing war in Gaza can be the beginning. James Jeffrey, the former U.S. envoy to Syria, said in a statement: "Moscow wants to benefit from Syria's bankrupt economic structure, and it wants to have loyal forces there. Tehran desires to be a dominant force in the region against the West, and the unresolved Syrian crisis has increased Turkey's concerns. Ankara does not want to leave Syria due to its security concerns. The issue of the PKK (The Kurdistan Workers' Party) is a significant issue for Turkey, and so are the refugees"[116].

Also, Jeffrey noted that Syria is one of the most dangerous issues in the Middle East and the world. And that Iran, Russia, the United States, Turkey, and Israel all have a say in this issue. In a televised interview on the NBC station after the U.S. withdrawal from Afghanistan, President Biden said, "Syria has become more dangerous than the Taliban. We must focus on the most critical threat." He meant the Chinese threat. However, American newspapers and think tanks, including the Washington Institute for the Near East, concluded that the Biden administration needs an unclouded vision for a solution in Syria. "Thanks to Russian and

---

[116] U.S. Envoy to Syria praises Idlib deal. By Chloe Cornish October 17, 2018. https://www.ft.com/content/de4427b0-d211-11e8-a9f2-7574db66bcd5.

Iranian support, the Syrian regime has progressively consolidated control over much of the territory since 2015. As of 2020, several hundred U.S. forces continued to support Syrian Democratic Forces (SDF) in northeast Syria, while Turkey-backed troops continued to hold off the regime in Idlib and occupy a slice of the border that it had occupied with the blessing of the United States in October 2019[117]."

Both the Obama and Trump administrations supported the United Nations Security Council Resolution 2254, which seeks to end the conflict through a new constitution and elections that would pave the way for Assad's exit. Russian and Chinese vetoes at the Security Council and the arrival of the Astana process to the United States' Geneva talks have hindered progress. Although Turkey is a NATO member and a long-time U.S. friend, it did not help counterbalance this move. Instead, it joined Russia and Iran in the Astana talks. Turkey's role in the region has undergone a significant transformation over the last two decades, moving from a stance of non-interference in Middle East affairs to an assertive and influential position. While Iran expanded its influence in the East, Turkey focused on the West, aspiring to join the European Union. It strategically maintained the East as a fallback option. However, the changing geopolitical landscape in the region

---

[117] RAND 2021 Study Report. Dalia Dasa Kaye, Linda Robinson, Jeffrey Martini, Nathan Vest, and Ashley L. Rhoads. "Reimagining U.S. Strategy in the Middle East: Sustainable Partnerships, Strategic Investments." RAND Corporation, Santa Monica, Calif, 2021, Page 56.

(MENA) after President Obama took office prompted Turkey to reassess its priorities. Under the leadership of President Recep Tayyip Erdogan and the Justice and Development Party, Turkey shifted its focus towards establishing a more substantial presence in the East. This strategic pivot is driven by Turkey's desire to enhance effectiveness and strength, particularly when Turkey perceives a pressing need for such a recalibration.

The U.S. and Conflict in Syria

"Summary, Conclusions, and Recommendations"

The potential benefits of achieving a decisive victory in the ongoing conflict in Syria for the United States are significant. This victory represents not just a strategic objective but also an opportunity to effectively tackle challenges posed by Russia and to strategically compete with China. The U.S. must assert its dominance and impose a strategic vision similar to its role following World War II. The conflict in Syria is a source of instability throughout the Middle East and contributes to tensions in both Ukraine and Taiwan.

Historically, controlling the seas and oceans was crucial to global dominance in World War I. In contrast, during World War II, control over Eurasia played a significant role in the outcome. In the current geopolitical landscape, U.S. strategy aims to dominate both the Indian and Pacific Oceans (referred to as the Indo-Pacific), with a strong emphasis on maritime control. Meanwhile, Russian President Vladimir Putin focuses on dominating Eurasia, while Chinese President Xi Jinping seeks to leverage both land and sea for

Chinese trade, demonstrating a comprehensive and strategic approach to global influence.

Mark Twain once said, "History does not repeat itself, but often rhymes." Europe (England and France) dominated the Middle East after World War I, and America (the United States) after World War II. Asia (Russia and China) hopes to benefit from World War III and assume such a role. Thus, resolving the regional and international conflict in Syria can bring stability to it and the other unstable countries in the region, fueled by the Syrian crisis, including Israel's ongoing conflict with Hamas in Gaza. It will also restore stability in Iraq and normalize Iran and Turkey's role in the region. All these can contribute significantly to resolving the Arab-Israeli conflict and easing the tension in the Middle East and the World. Therefore, the United States can only prevent World War III, which will benefit Russia and China by promoting a balanced geopolitical climate in Syria and the Middle East.

Chapter 8: As the Sand Shifts Reevaluating the U.S. Strategy in the Middle East

To evaluate the U.S.'s success in managing the five challenges identified in previous chapters, the author conducted a survey comprising fifty-two participants—36 from the Middle East and sixteen from the United States. The findings revealed that 78% of respondents expressed skepticism, doubting the U.S.'s ability to address these complex issues effectively. Nevertheless, 22% remained optimistic, providing a hopeful perspective on the U.S.'s potential for success. The survey also uncovered stark differences in perceptions between American and Middle Eastern respondents regarding the global confrontations with China and Russia. Over 85% of Americans expressed confidence in the U.S.'s ability to prevail against these nations. In stark contrast, a similar percentage of Middle Eastern respondents believed that the U.S. would yield to the pressures of China and Russia and withdraw from the Middle East. While the author recognizes the survey's limited scope and urges caution in drawing broad conclusions from its small, diverse sample, he asserts that there is still a path forward. By adopting a fresh strategy in the Middle East, redefining its global role, and fostering national unity, the U.S. can strengthen its position in the ongoing worldwide conflict and work toward a more favorable outcome.

Conclusions and Recommendations

We cannot change our history, but we can certainly shape our future. Seventy-seven years after the end of World War II and over thirty years since the Cold War concluded, our world faces renewed geopolitical tensions that demand our attention. While the past is unchangeable, we must take urgent action to prevent a potential third world war. Historically, global conflicts have originated in Europe, leading to widespread consequences in the Middle East. Today, we are witnessing conflicts that started as a proxy war in Syria in 2014, escalating into the conflict in Ukraine in Eastern Europe in 2022, and now the ongoing crisis in Gaza since October 7, 2023. Without timely and effective intervention, these tensions risk spiraling into larger-scale confrontations, impacting not just these regions but the entire globe. It is imperative that we act decisively to foster peace and stability.

Winning local battles, such as the ongoing conflict in Gaza against Hamas, does not effectively address the deeper issues plaguing the Middle East. Yet, resolving these regional conflicts could be pivotal in averting a potential world war. To achieve lasting peace and stability globally, we must engage in substantial international efforts to prevent further escalation. The United States has a critical role to play; it must reassess its approach in the Middle East and lead by setting a positive example—prioritizing diplomacy and cooperation over military action.

Since the end of the Cold War, U.S. policy in the Middle East, spanning successive administrations, has faced challenges and criticism for its perceived lack of tangible results and the absence of cohesive strategies[118]. Persistent issues, such as the Arab-Israeli conflict and the adversarial stance of Iran, remain unresolved. The Syrian crisis has been compounded by the failure of President Obama's Middle East Approach, leading to a power vacuum that has prompted Russia to strengthen its position in Syria and the broader Middle East outreach areas, such as Central Africa. Simultaneously, China has seized opportunities to expand its influence in the region. However, the complexity of historical, cultural, and geopolitical factors, coupled with the region's dynamic nature, underscores the difficulty of crafting and implementing effective long-term policies. Nonetheless, the US cannot abandon the Middle East and leave it in a vacuum that its competitors, Russia and China, fill. However, the United States cannot face new challenges with an old strategy. It must reevaluate its strategy in the Middle East and recalibrate the related foreign policies. The author contends that a successful strategy necessitates a clear, well-defined vision for the future and realistic, achievable, and timely objectives. However, the United States lacks such a vision for the Middle East and, notably, has not implemented a New Middle East approach that aligns with the changing geopolitical landscape. This absence of a novel approach underscores the need for a revised strategy. In response, the author proposes a selective, creative, and

---

[118] US Policy and Strategy in the Middle East. James Jeffery. The Washington Institute for Near East Policy, December 14, 2107. Retrieved from: U.S. Policy and Strategy in the Middle East | The Washington Institute.

sensitive (SCSS) overarching strategy to reassess the U.S. strategy for the Middle East. This strategy emphasizes three fundamental principles:

1. **Selective:** In an increasingly multipolar world, the United States must adapt its geopolitical strategy, moving beyond the notion of being the sole superpower. A more prudent relief approach involves identifying and cultivating only regions of influence that align with U.S. interests and enhance its geostrategic leverage that copes with the emerging Russian challenge and competition with China. The Middle East stands out as a pivotal area for prioritization. This region is not only rich in natural resources but also serves as a critical crossroads for global trade and security. By fostering strong partnerships and alliances in this area, the U.S. can tap into economic opportunities, enhance energy security, and counterbalance the influence of adversarial powers seeking to expand their reach. Moreover, focusing on the Middle East allows the U.S. to engage with a diverse array of cultures and political systems, fostering stability and promoting democratic values. Supporting reform and development initiatives in the region can contribute to long-term peace and security, which are undeniably in U.S. interests.

- To successfully navigate this complex landscape, the U.S. must adopt a strategy that is both flexible and responsive to the dynamic geopolitical realities of the 21st century. By strategically engaging in the Middle East, the U.S. can strengthen its position on the world stage and ensure that it continues to play a significant role in shaping global affairs. This deliberate, regionally focused strategy is not merely an option; it is a necessity for the future of U.S. foreign policy as the U.S faces up to Russia and China.

2. **Creative:** The world has changed dramatically, and it is essential that the United States re-evaluates its approach to international relations and conflict resolution. The old, militarized strategies that once dominated our foreign policy have become outdated and incompatible with today's advanced technology and evolving geopolitical realities. It is time to forge a new pathway — one that is innovative, strategic, and reflective of the American people's desire for a more peaceful approach. Americans are weary of endless wars, military interventions, and the immense financial burden they impose, particularly in regions like the Middle East. We must recognize that the landscape of global conflict is shifting. Our strategy needs to evolve to reflect this reality by prioritizing technology over traditional military might. By leveraging advanced tools such as cyberspace capabilities and Artificial Intelligence (AI), we can gain power advantages while minimizing the human and financial costs associated with conventional military operations. Adopting a strategy that emphasizes technological prowess over militarization does not mean abandoning our commitment to security. Rather, it

represents a more effective and sustainable way to address conflicts. By focusing on creative, strategic solutions and fostering innovation in our approach to international relations, we can meet our goals without the heavy toll of previous interventions. However, this shift requires more than just a change in tactics; it necessitates the development of relevant policies to ensure that our technology-driven approach is responsible and controlled. We must establish guidelines that govern the use of these powerful tools, ensuring they are employed ethically and effectively. In conclusion, the United States stands at a crossroads. By embracing a new strategy that prioritizes technological advancements over militarization, we can lead by example in the global arena, responding to conflicts with ingenuity rather than aggression. This is not just a pragmatic shift; it is a moral imperative. Let us invest in a more peaceful and prosperous future, creating a global landscape where dialogue and diplomacy take precedence over conflict and chaos.

3. **Sensitive:** The past strategy of the U.S. focusing on investing in governments and regimes has not yielded the desired resolution to the complex challenges in the Middle East. It is time to pivot towards a more effective approach that prioritizes the well-being of the people and fosters social mobility. By investing in initiatives that promote economic growth and social development, we can create a more stable and prosperous environment

that aligns with U.S. interests. A people-oriented strategy not only addresses immediate needs but also lays the groundwork for sustainable development. We need long-term initiatives that enable individuals to thrive, driving grassroots change and reducing the allure of extremism born from disenfranchisement. Empowering local communities through education, entrepreneurship, and public health can lead to a more resilient society, which benefits U.S. interests in terms of security and economic ties. Furthermore, by shifting our focus from corrupt governance structures to directly uplifting individuals, we have the opportunity to rebuild trust and foster goodwill among populations that have often felt overlooked. This can lead to stronger partnerships forged into mutual respect and shared goals. Sustainable progress in the Middle East hinges on our ability to connect with the people, not just the regimes.

- In conclusion, embracing a strategy that centers on social mobility and economic empowerment is not only ethically sound but also strategically advantageous. It is time for the U.S. to lead with compassion and foresight, investing in the future of the people in the Middle East for a more stable and prosperous region.

However, the proposed strategy acknowledges the challenges, including political divisions among United States lawmakers and the complexities associated with an election year. Nevertheless, only a U.S. global strategy can be meaningful and practical with a cohesive plan and supportive foreign policies adopted by the U.S. Congress to implement it, which should be a national strategy regardless of the administration in power.

Recalibrating U.S. Foreign Policies

In the past, the United States could win most wars, including the Cold War, but was unable to establish lasting peace and stability afterward. In the post-Cold War era, global dynamics have shifted significantly. However, Vietnam, despite its unification, continues to face economic and social challenges, the Korean Peninsula remains divided and on the verge of war between the two sides, and Afghanistan is in turmoil. Despite the dissolution of the Soviet Union, NATO has expanded into Eastern Europe, approaching Russia's borders. China actively pursues reunification with Taiwan, while the Middle East remains a focal point of global competition. The UN Security Council, composed of the five permanent members entrusted with maintaining the world order after World War II and during the Cold War, was hindered by its veto power and left the world in a state of disorder as it strove for a new world order. Considering these changes, the following overarching conclusions and recommendations are proposed for a strategic approach:

Internationally:

- The focus has shifted from Europe to Asia, and the global conflict is changing from the East-West conflict during the Cold

War with the Soviet Union to a South-North dynamic as China emerges as the main competitor to the U.S.

- To win the ongoing global conflict spanning multiple continents, the United States must solidify its presence in North America and safeguard its interests in Central and South America, which are its backyard.

- U.S. effective foreign policies require not only strong leadership from the U.S. president and administration but also the active involvement and responsibility of a united U.S. Congress.

- The U.S. ought to learn from historical events and avoid repeating past mistakes in international relations. Drawing parallels between historical situations, such as the aftermath of World War II and the Cold War, can offer insights into the potential consequences of failed diplomacy and the importance of negotiating fair and sustainable agreements. In the aftermath of World War II, the once-stable international order crumbled, plunging the world into chaos. Hence, the U.S. and its competitors must prioritize negotiations over conflict to forge a new, more cohesive global order. This negotiation-centric approach is crucial for saving lives, advancing humanity, and effectively addressing urgent challenges such as climate change. Emphasizing dialogue over war is essential, as it enables the international community to construct a framework for a New World Order collaboratively. This approach aims to promote stability, foster cooperation, and facilitate sustainable redevelopment on a global scale. Rather than resorting to military action with devastating consequences, diplomatic discussions offer an avenue for resolving disputes and shaping a more harmonious world, drawing on President Nixon's strategy to ease tensions with the Soviet Union and open relations with China. A strategy that prompted President Nixon to visit both countries in 1972. In any case, the U.S. should prevent a cold war with China or Russia. The U.S. still has the military leverage to gain momentum with diplomacy. In any case, the U.S. should avoid a cold war with China or Russia. The U.S. still has the military leverage to gain momentum with diplomacy. Thus, it can adopt President Theodor Roosevelt's Approach: "Speaking softly and carrying a big stick, you will go far." Roosevelt described his style of foreign policy as "the exercise of intelligent forethought and of decisive action sufficiently far in advance of any likely crisis"[119].

- Crucially, all involved parties, including the U.S., must be willing to make concessions to reach a fair and equitable agreement. The potential losses incurred through a negotiated settlement are significantly outweighed by the catastrophic consequences of engaging in warfare. The adage "there are no winners in war" underscores the futility of military conflicts and emphasizes the importance of seeking peaceful resolutions through diplomatic channels.

---

[119] David McCullagh (1977). *The Path Between the Seas: The Creation of the Panama Canal, 1870–1914*. Simon and Schuster, P.382.

- By prioritizing negotiations and embracing a cooperative mindset, the international community can pave the way for a more stable, secure, and sustainable future for this and subsequent generations. This collaborative effort mitigates the immediate threats posed by conflicts and sets the stage for addressing long-term challenges, such as climate change, which affects the entire planet.

- The proliferation of nuclear weapons and the potential intersection with artificial intelligence (AI) underscores the need for global disarmament and responsible AI governance. The growing number of countries possessing nuclear weapons, combined with the potential integration of artificial intelligence into military systems, raises significant concerns and requires serious attention by all involved global parties.

Regionally, in the Middle East

The historical U.S. Middle East strategy primarily concentrated on engaging with governments and did not emphasize presenting the U.S. as a governance model. A proposed shift in strategy suggests prioritizing investments in the Region's people. Despite the Arab Spring's failure to overthrow dictatorial regimes, it highlighted the people as a potent and influential factor in the Region that cannot be ignored. In a study conducted by RAND Institute, the researchers concluded that: "After more than a decade of a popular uprising against corrupt, repressive, incompetent governance in various Middle Eastern countries, no U.S. strategy is likely to succeed without considering the well-being and dignity of the Region's people"[120]. Hence, the author wants to stress the following recommendations for the proposed new strategic approach for the U.S. in the Middle East and the outreaching Region.

- Adopt a regional strategic approach and its keen implementation in the Middle East, inspired by President Obama's Middle East and North Africa Approach. This approach offers a promising vision, serving as a beacon of hope and a foundation for addressing the region's current challenges. However, success hinges on practical and well-executed implementation measures encompassing diplomatic initiatives, economic cooperation, and security measures. A nuanced understanding of the area's intricate geopolitical landscape must embrace this approach.

- To effectively address the region's challenges, it is crucial to move beyond supporting outdated concepts such as occupational powers and religious states, recognizing that they defy contemporary logic. Instead, the focus should be on fostering an environment where people of diverse religions and ethnic backgrounds can coexist harmoniously, drawing inspiration from historical precedents in the cradle of civilization and the birthplace of religions. The realization that

---

[120] RAND 2021 Study Report. Dalia Dasa Kaye, Linda Robinson, Jeffrey Martini, Nathan Vest, and Ashley L. Rhoads. "Reimagining U.S. Strategy in the Middle East: Sustainable Partnerships, Strategic Investments." RAND Corporation, Santa Monica, Calif, 2021, Page 108.

people with different religious and ethnic backgrounds have coexisted peacefully in the region throughout history is a testament to the potential for harmony. This historical precedent should inspire contemporary efforts to build bridges of understanding and collaboration between the Middle East and the West's diverse communities.

- The key to success lies in diplomatic initiatives that prioritize dialogue and cooperation among all countries in the Middle East. Strategic partnerships and economic collaboration can be powerful drivers of positive change, promoting regional stability and prosperity. Simultaneously, well-crafted security measures are necessary to address immediate threats and build trust among nations.

- The success of a strategic approach in the Middle East requires a concerted effort to break free from outdated paradigms and embrace a vision of unity, cooperation, and shared prosperity. With the will to forge a path of collaboration, we can build a more stable and peaceful future for the region.

- Recognizing the geostrategic significance of the Middle East is essential for the U.S. as it faces the pressing challenges posed by Russia and China. Following the withdrawal from Afghanistan and the potential loss of influence in Central Asia (in the former Soviet Union states), the United States must prioritize maintaining robust connections with Pakistan. Additionally, fostering a strategic partnership with India becomes imperative. This approach ensures the U.S. retains influence across the entire region, spanning from North Africa and the

Mediterranean Basin to the borders of China, with access to the Arabian Sea and the Indian and Pacific Oceans, as depicted in Fig. 9 on the map below.

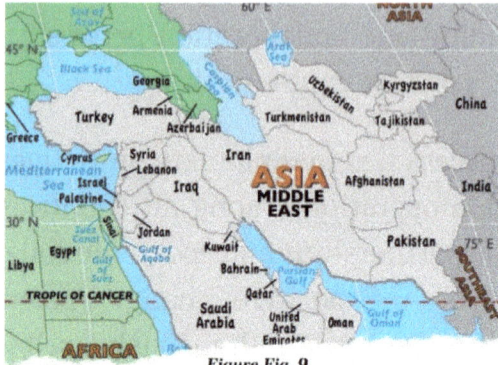

Figure Fig. 9.

Figure 9: The Greater Middle East Map

- The India-Europe Trade Route that the United States sponsored in the last G-20 in Mumbai, India, meeting held on 23-25 May 2023, is to counter China's Silk roads outlined in the BRI, and is only a short step in an exceedingly long way to effectively compete with China's RBI.

- The India-Europe Route passes through the UAE, Saudi Arabia, Jordan, and Israel[121], as shown in Fig. 10.

---

[121]At G-20, Biden announced the ambitious corridor connecting India and Europe. By Matt Viser and Karishma Mehrotra. The Washington Post. Published September 9, 2023. Retrieved from: G-20 leaders announce rail and shipping corridor connecting India and Europe - The Washington Post

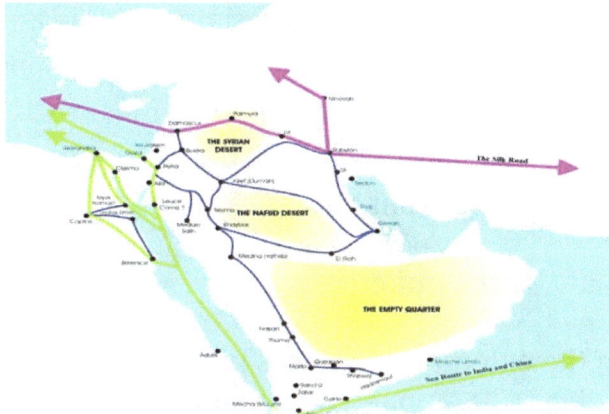

Figure Fig. 10. A map of the India-Europe Middle East Trade Route.

Figure 10: The Indo-Europe Middle East Route

- However, this route undermines the Suez Canal in Egypt, a U.S. ally, and the gateway to North Africa. Also, it alienates other countries in the region critical to the new U.S. Middle East strategy, including Iran, Iraq, Turkey, Syria, and Lebanon. Besides, a straightforward road cannot strategically compete with a network of roads in the region and to Europe, Africa, and South America[122].

- The U.S.'s new Middle East strategy must pay attention to critical geostrategic areas in Asia and Africa, with more than

---

[122] New US-backed India-Middle East trade route to challenge China's ambitions. By Nadeen Ebrahim, CNN. Updated 11:10 AM EDT, Mon. September 11, 2023.

75% of the global population residing in Asia and Africa, both rich in natural resources and possessing a substantial labor force; China has turned its attention to these regions. Russia has also joined, establishing a foothold in this expansive and strategically significant area[123].

Nationally, in the United States

- Despite the external challenges posed by growing competition from China, the Russian challenge to American global dominance, and the rise of other international powers, the most significant threats to the United States today stem from internal divisions and societal issues. These challenges, reminiscent of the post-Civil War era, include deep political and social divisions, racial injustice, social inequality, and questions about the effectiveness of domestic governance institutions.

- The current state of the United States reflects a level of internal strife not seen since the aftermath of the Civil War. President Abraham Lincoln had warned about the potential for internal enemies, and today's divisions manifest in political

---

[123] The world population is expected to reach eight billion as the growth rate slows. The United Nations News, 11 July 2022. Retrieved from: World population to reach 8 billion this year, as growth rate slows | UN News.

polarization, debates over systemic racism, and ideological rifts[124].

- The country is contending with issues of racial injustice, inequality, and systemic discrimination, which emphasize the urgent need for a national collective effort by American politicians in all three branches of government to address these critical concerns that the U.S. Faces. Challenges to democratic norms and institutions, such as concerns about election integrity and security, political polarization, and threats to democratic values, are perceived as unprecedented. The very foundations of the democratic system, characterized by political tolerance and checks and balances, are being assessed. It is essential to recognize that the greatness of the United States is not solely derived from its military might. Instead, it is rooted in its democratic system, characterized by political tolerance and adequate checks and balances. The nation's identity as the land of opportunity, where diversity can flourish, has also contributed to its strength. Leading by the force of example, rather than mere military power, has historically defined the United States.

---

[124] Michael Dimock and Richard Wike. America is exceptional in its political divide. Pew Research Center. Published on November 13, 2020. Retrieved from: America is exceptional in its political divide | Pew Research Center.

As the nation navigates a changing global landscape, it is crucial to heed the lessons of history and avoid getting entangled in a new World War, whether hot or cold. The United States must lead by the power of example, not by the example of power. The endurance of a country lies not only in its military might, but also in the strength of its ideals and its ability to address its internal challenges. Thus, the United States must remain true to its democratic principles, a beacon of opportunity and diversity, to shape a new world order and continue to be a superpower in the 21st century.

Picking up Where We Left Off with Biden and Trump

It has been two years since this book was initially released. During the last two years of President Biden's term and a year since President Trump was elected for a second term, many significant developments have occurred in the Middle East and around the world, the most notable of which is the fall of the Syrian Regime and the drastic changes that have been taking place ever since. Also, the dynamic development of the war in Gaza. Therefore, it was necessary to go back and pick up where we left off. And cover the most momentous events of this period, complementing the book's first release and confirming its conclusions and forecasts.

As forecast in the book's initial release, President Joe Biden was expected to be a transitional one-term president. Nonetheless, he decided to run and proceeded with his campaign before being forced to reverse his decision under pressure from senior members of the Democratic Party, in particular, and from Americans in general. The author was among the first to urge President Biden not to run in a private letter. The argument presented in the appeal to

President Biden not to run was not to make way for his Vice President, Kamala Harris, because the author was aware of the difficulty she would face in reaching the White House, as stated in previous chapters. Instead, the appeal to President Biden focused primarily on the need for him to be freed from the responsibilities of running and the requirements and conditions of financial backers, so he can devote his time and energy in the remainder of his presidency to saving the world from an inevitable Third World War, and also to keeping the United States from the continued political and social decline the country had reached at the time. Given his age and extensive political experience in foreign affairs, he could have achieved tangible success if he had tried. So, he would have been among the great American presidents who faced similar challenges and achieved outstanding accomplishments, such as George Washington, the Liberator and first president of the United States, and Abraham Lincoln, the emancipator of enslaved people who preserved the unity and cohesion of the American Union. Franklin Roosevelt also led the United States out of the Great Depression. He led the country to victory in World War II, thereby establishing it as a superpower thereafter. So, for President Biden to prevent World War III and develop the foundations for the new world order, as I explained, it was imperative to address three key issues that have been pending since the end of the Cold War. Leaving them open without solutions provided and implemented by the United States would lead to a Third World War. These issues include halting the Russian–Ukrainian war and preventing its expansion to other regions in Eastern Europe. Another critical issue is stopping the war launched by Israel against Gaza after the events of October 7, 2023. This war was the cumulative result of unresolved Middle Eastern issues, especially the war in Syria and the Palestinian issue, and the region has plunged into chaos and religious and sectarian extremism after the occupation of Iraq in 2003. The third issue that must be addressed and resolved is the Taiwan issue and the settlement of the conflict with China over the South China Sea and East Asia, as discussed in previous chapters.

Although President Biden eventually withdrew from the presidential race and devoted himself to important foreign and domestic issues, he failed to achieve any significant accomplishments in any of them. He was unable to capitalize on the events of October 7 to bring down Netanyahu's right-wing government, thereby paving the way for another government that could accept the two-state solution and satisfy the Saudi condition for normalization with Israel. He was also unable to prevent Netanyahu from launching a devastating attack on Gaza. This issue has become disastrous, a burden, and a responsibility for the United States and the international community. Before that, President Biden was unable to stop Russia's attack on Ukraine before it started or provide the assistance required to win the war, despite all the aid provided by the United States and European Union countries. The Biden administration also made no notable progress with China on the outstanding issues between the two countries, despite his face-to-face meeting with Chinese President Xi Jinping in San Francisco, United States. During the meeting, Xi reaffirmed China's unwavering decision to annex Taiwan, whether through peaceful means or by force.

President Biden left the White House, leaving many pressing issues unresolved for his successor, including the war in Syria, which poses a significant challenge and holds the key to resolving many of the Middle East's problems due to its close connection to all regional issues. The Syrian arena is considered a regional and international arena of influence. As mentioned in previous chapters, ending the war in Syria by the United States will give it the upper hand in resolving the conflict in the region and prevent it from escalating into a third world war. It will also enable it to have a considerable influence in establishing a new world order, due to China's economic competition in the region and Russia's military presence there.

The winner of the 2024 presidential election was not a Trumpian, as predicted in the book's first release early in 2024. However, the winner was Trump himself. The primary slogan raised by President Trump in his 2024 campaign was preventing a third world war. He pledged to end the Russian–Ukrainian war within 24 hours. He also boasted that if he had been the President, this war would not have occurred. He also pledged to stop the war in Gaza and achieve normalization between Israel and the Arab states, specifically with Saudi Arabia. He also promised to impose a nuclear agreement on Iran, which his predecessor, President Biden, was unable to enforce or even revive the deal signed with Iran by the Obama administration in 2015, which the Trump administration had canceled during its first term in 2018.

To his credit, President Trump swiftly began formulating and implementing a transformative strategy for the Middle East immediately following his victory in the November 5, 2024, election. Remarkably, he did not wait for his official inauguration in early 2025; he took decisive action right away. Central to his approach was the prioritization of critical issues, commencing with the urgent need to resolve the Syrian crisis—an initiative thoroughly outlined in Chapter 7 of this book. President-elect Trump took bold steps, coordinating effectively with the outgoing Biden administration, demonstrating a commitment to bipartisan collaboration. His strategy garnered the support of Israel, Turkey, and Russia, who collectively recognized the necessity of dismantling the entrenched Syrian regime that had persisted for over fifty years. This coalition skillfully leveraged the dismantling of Iranian-backed forces in Syria, particularly following the strategic elimination of key Hezbollah leaders, including Secretary-General Hassan Nasrallah. The culmination of these efforts came **on December 8, 2024,** when the Syrian regime collapsed and President Bashar al-Assad fled to Moscow, just a month after Trump's election, and over a month before entering the White House for the second time. This pivotal moment in Syria paved the way right away for considerable progress in Lebanon, where, under American encouragement—specifically from President-elect Trump and with the backing of France and Saudi Arabia—a consensus emerged among Lebanese factions to elect Army Commander General Joseph Aoun as President. This new leadership was the catalyst for forming a government under Judge Nawaf Salam, marking a critical step toward the implementation of UN Resolution 1701. This resolution mandates the withdrawal of Hezbollah forces to the north of the AL-Litany River and the clarification of the border with Israel—a goal that President Biden had long sought but was unable to achieve before his departure from the White House. Such developments not only represent a significant diplomatic triumph but also lay the groundwork for a renewed, constructive deal with Iran concerning its nuclear program, especially in light of the dramatic shifts occurring in the region. It is worth noting that a similar approach was initially proposed by President Obama in 2012 after the outbreak of the Syrian Revolution. However, it faced outright rejection from then-Prime Minister Netanyahu, as it conflicted with Israel's interests at the time. Now, we stand on the cusp of a new era, where collaborative efforts and strategic foresight can reshape the future of the Middle East for the better.

President Biden left the White House and President Trump reentered it **on January 20, 2025**. Despite the withdrawal of Hezbollah's armed forces to the north of the AL-Litany River as the UN Resolution No. 1701 stipulates, they have not yet surrendered their weapons to the Lebanese Government, as required by the No. 1959 Resolution. In the meantime, Israel still occupies the strategic Five Points area in southern Lebanon and has not withdrawn from it as stipulated in the agreement, as the same resolutions require. The border between Israel and Lebanon has not yet been demarcated, despite a year of President Trump's second term. The situation in Syria has not been stabilized as President Trump intended, despite a year having passed since the fall of the Syrian regime and the fleeing of President al-Assad. Instead, the process of dividing Syria like international and regional spheres of influence has begun. Also, the peace agreement and border demarcation between Syria and Israel, as President Trump had hoped, have yet to be signed. In September of 2025, Syrian interim president Ahmad al-Sharaa addressed the United Nations General Assembly under pressure from President Trump, who was desperate to win the Nobel Peace Prize. However, the security agreement between Israel and Syria was not signed in a media-like ceremony on the sidelines of the 80th session of the United Nations, as President Trump had hoped and expected. Such a situation is because Israeli Prime Minister Benjamin Netanyahu repeatedly changes the conditions, making them impossible and unachievable. He is doing so to impose the necessary impasse for his government to survive and remain in power until the Israeli elections in September 2026. He is doing the same with all other regional issues related to Syria, Lebanon, Palestine, and Iran. He believes that, after the **October 7 attack**, Israel is in a position of strength, and all its opponents are in a position of weakness, allowing him to expand and implement the Zionist dream of a Greater Israel from the Euphrates to the Nile. This intention of Israel in itself has begun to pose an existential threat to all regional states, including Egypt and Saudi Arabia, as well as Iran, Turkey, and Pakistan. These countries have found themselves forced to build alliances among themselves to confront Israel's dangerous project. Their move includes the Saudi-Pakistani military partnership, as well as the Egyptian-Turkish agreement on a defense strategy and joint military maneuvers. These moves are also in addition to Iran's developing strategic alliances with Russia and China.

President Trump, in his quest to reshape the global landscape to his vision, has struggled to rein in the impulsiveness and recklessness exhibited by his ally, Netanyahu. This challenge has intensified, particularly after Trump's inability to effectively engage with Putin and temper his aggressive posture over the war in Ukraine. While Trump did broker a truce to halt the violence in Gaza, this achievement, though notable, falls short of the threshold required for the Nobel Peace Prize. A temporary ceasefire in Gaza cannot serve as a panacea for the longstanding conflict in the Middle East; it demands a just and comprehensive peace plan to foster enduring stability. Furthermore, without addressing the root causes and broader regional dynamics, the truce risks merely postponing the inevitable escalation into a wider conflict, potentially endangering not only the region but the world at large. This volatile backdrop is exacerbated by Trump's initiation of a trade war against numerous countries, particularly China, which diverts attention and resources from diplomatic efforts crucial for lasting peace. To genuinely secure a safer and more stable world, President Trump must prioritize an integrated approach that encompasses dialogue, negotiation, and a sincere commitment to justice in the Middle East and beyond. Only then can we hope to avert a catastrophic escalation and move towards a future rooted in cooperation and mutual respect.

In the final conclusion, the stakes could not be higher for the future of global stability. An honest and pragmatic reassessment of our geopolitical strategies is not merely preferable but essential. Without addressing the legacy issues tied to World War II and adapting our approaches in light of the contemporary landscape, we risk igniting a world conflict that could spiral out of control, wreaking havoc on nations and people alike. As we stand on the brink of potential global upheaval, it is crucial that this, or any future American administration, prioritizes the development of a new, intelligent, and practical strategy—one that moves beyond outdated frameworks and acknowledges the shifting dynamics of power. This strategy must advocate for a thoughtful engagement with key global players, pivoting towards smart diplomacy and genuine partnerships. A collaborative effort among the United States, China, Russia, and the European Union is vital in crafting a new world order built on mutual understanding and respect. The existing structures of the United Nations Security Council and NATO have become relics, hampering our ability to respond effectively to today's challenges. By redefining these institutions and embracing a more inclusive approach, we can foster peace that goes beyond mere treaties, truly addressing the root causes of conflict. Furthermore, the enduring issue of the Israeli-Palestinian conflict requires fresh thinking. A one-state solution that embodies the principle of coexistence for both people offers a pragmatic path forward. It aligns with the need for a unified Middle East that can stand resilient against extrinsic pressures, particularly from global powers like China. In this new era, we must recognize that our security is intertwined with the stability of global partners. By championing a strategy that cultivates cooperation rather than division, we stand a better chance of achieving lasting peace and safeguarding the future for generations to come. It is time for bold action and transformative thinking—our collective survival depends on it.

Index

Abbreviations

AUKUS	Australia, UK, and U.S Indo-Pacific Alliance 99
BRI	Belt and Road Initiative 39,88,89,97,140
GCC	Gulf Cooperative Council (Gulf States). 47,73,121
IRG	Iranian Revolutionary Guard 5
ISIS	Islamic State of Iraq and Syria 2,5,33,37,38,108,118
JCPOA	Joint Cooperative Plan of Action 68
MAGA	Make America Great Again 5
MENA	Middle East and North Africa 2,20,25,26,71,89,90,125
NATO	North Atlantic Treaty Organization 75,79,80,81,86,87,124,134,152
PLO	Palestinian Liberation Organization 48
PNA	Palestinian National Authority 48
PRC	People Republic of China 89,90
UAE	United Arab Emirates 75,89,96,109,140
UN	United Nations 17,46,134,148,149

Accords, Agreements, and Treaties

Oslo Accords 18,42,47,48,40,55,58

Sikes-Picot Agreement 3

1974 Israel-Egypt Military Disengagement Agreement 27

1974 Israel-Syria Military Disengagement Agreement 27

Camp David 1979 Peace Treaty 47

Balfour Declaration 3,19,40,42

Gaza 8,18,19,42,48,49, 53,55,57,92,123,128,145,147,151

Hamas 60, 126, 128

Hezbollah 30, 65, 122, 148

Houthis 66

United Nations Resolutions

Resolution N0. # 181 adopted in 1947 requiring mandatory partitioning of Palestine for Arabs and Jewish. 42,52

Resolution NO. 242 (Land for Peace adopted after 1967 war) 17,44.

Resolution NO. 338, adopted after 1973, called for ceasefire. 17,46

Resolution NO. 339 subsequent to resolution 17,46

Resolution NO. 340 is subsequent to resolution 17,46

Resolution NO. # 2254 adopted in 20015 calling for ceasefire and political settlement in Syria. 30,124

Wars

World War I (194-1918) 12,19,98

World War II (1039-1945) 1,4,26,120,128,134,135,151

1948 War (1948) 56,57

1956 War (Suez War) 13,44

1967 War (Six-day War) 17,28,42,43,44,45,

1973 War (Yom Kapoor War) 17,28,45,46,80

Iraq-Iran War (1980-1988) 19.

Gulf War (1991 Desert Storm) 1,5,20

War on Terrorism (After September 11, 2001) 20,23,38,74,75,141

Invasion of Afghanistan (2001) 70

Invasion of Iraq (2003) 72,120

www.ingramcontent.com/pod-product-compliance
Lightning Source LLC
Chambersburg PA
CBHW060231030426
42335CB00014B/1404